High Altitude Leadership:

Small Steps to Get You to the Top of Big Mountains

Steve Camkin

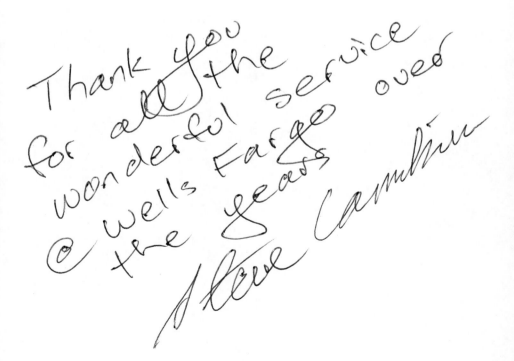

Thank you for all the wonderful service @ Wells Fargo over the years

Steve Camkin

Table of Contents

Acknowledgements

To Mum and Dad for my first leadership lessons.

To some especially good leaders – Tom, Carol, Shane, and Clem – who have been not only inspirational, but also great mentors.

To all the leaders I have worked for. I learned things from both good and bad leaders – how to follow, how to lead, what to strive for, and compassion for leaders' challenges.

To those I have led by choice or otherwise. Thank you for your grace with my mistakes as I learned.

To those who lead every day, often under the radar, to make the world a better place. Thank you for stepping up.

To those who lead without a title and often without recognition through service to others. Thank you for your silent contributions.

To my partners on outdoor adventures through the years. Thank you for sharing the wilderness with me, for helping me appreciate it even more, and for keeping me safe in spite of myself.

To the sirdars, cooks, guides, and others in Borneo, Nepal, Tanzania, Bolivia, Ecuador, New Zealand, Alaska, and other places around the globe I've travelled to. Thank you for your wisdom, your skills, your love of life, and for hauling thousands of kilos of food and equipment through jungles, across crevasses, and up icy slopes so that I could selfishly enjoy the world.

To those who I haven't named but who contributed stories. Thank you for your candor and generosity.

To Sunniva, Rebecca, and Barbara. Thank you for your help in shaping my thoughts through your thoughtful and persistent editing and guidance.

Introduction

I recently sat, awestruck, watching *Meru*, a documentary film about three climbers' big-wall alpine climb to 21,850 feet. Physically, the three climbers battled the effects of altitude, hauled 200-pound bags of gear up incredibly steep faces of rock, and weathered storms suspended in a small porta-ledge (hanging tent) with thousands of feet of exposure. Emotionally, they dealt with fear, past failures, and how to build trust between team members in an environment where the decisions and actions had immediate, and very real consequences.

The film left me stunned by the climbers' performance but simultaneously depressed as I pondered the scale of my accomplishments by comparison. I have skydived, but my friend Rex is pushing the boundaries of jet pack flying. I ran my first marathon in 2 hours and 58 minutes with no training runs greater than 50 minutes, but friends from Europe have completed the Ultra-Trail Du Mont-Blanc (168 kilometers, 9600 meters of elevation gain, 40 hours average completion time). I have climbed the Seven Summits, but others have done that without oxygen and in far better style.

It's true that I worked for Outward Bound and other organizations for a number of years, leading people in wilderness situations, but even then there were much better skiers, rafters, and climbers than me. And yet my friends, family, and co-workers have kept pushing me to put my experiences down on digital paper.

So what do I have to offer? This book is an amateur adventurer's view on how to learn from your personal adventures (outdoors or in general life) and bring the lessons back to where they are most useful – at work, with your family, and in your community. Through my years of adventures, and on a sometimes wandering career path, one thread of continuity has been my interest in uncovering how experiences in one part of our lives can help us be more effective in other aspects of our lives.

While there are technical lessons to be learned from being on the cutting edge of any pursuit, for most of us, knowledge that is transferable to the real world can be gained through lower levels of challenge. We know, for example, that the extreme breathing skills used by record-setting free divers and high-altitude climbers are a key factor in their high performance, but we can easily apply the principles and some of the techniques at the office to re-energize during a mid-afternoon slump.

We all have adventures of differing scales every day. Talk to anyone who has raised kids, struggled with cancer, coached a soccer team, or tried to start a business.

But it doesn't have to be just the big adventures that teach us. Life and the outdoors offer a range of challenging experiences. Rock climbers, for example, grade terrain from Class I, which are easy, relatively flat trails, to Class V, which are extremely challenging faces where ropes and technical gear are required. It can be hard to crawl out of a sleeping bag for a snow climb at 1 a.m. when the temperature is minus 20 degrees Fahrenheit, and the wind is whipping, stinging ice into your face, but it can also be hard to avoid shutting off the alarm at 5 a.m. when you have been up all night with sick kids, and you are facing a tough day at work. It's mostly the degree of difficulty that differs.

There are things to be learned from both real life and adventure situations. What I have seen from 35 years of working with businesses, nonprofits, churches, the military, and groups as diverse as Vietnam Veterans, the visually impaired, and youth at risk is this: We don't share our stories with others frequently enough so that they can learn, and we can build connections with others in an increasingly disconnected world.

We all have many stories to tell, but we usually don't take the time to reflect on and learn from our stories and adventures. We often just cope with things and move on, not learning enough to build our capacity for managing future challenges effectively. Our failure to learn means we suffer rather than thrive when similar experiences repeat themselves. Organizations do it too. *Failure to Learn* was the name of a report that looked at the tragic consequences of failure to learn at BP through a series of incidents that culminated in a major oil spill and tragic loss of life.

The following chapters outline stories, principles, and lessons in life and leadership gleaned from a wide variety of expeditions and adventures on all seven continents over 35 years. While the focus of this book is on business leadership, the lessons apply to anyone wanting to be a better leader of themselves, peers, family, or community organizations. The stories are drawn from mountaineering, sailing, white-water rafting, caving, SCUBA, surfing, mountain biking, skydiving, rock climbing, and other outdoor activities.

The outdoors, and the adventures that take place there, can be a powerful learning medium. While the lessons in the coming chapters are primarily from settings in the outdoors, the leadership skills we can learn from all of life's adventures can serve us well in other parts of our lives. Hopefully, this book will refresh some of your own life and leadership experiences – and spark some new thinking about them.

Here are some of the trails we will explore:

- Why you choose to lead others
- Developing new leadership styles
- Selecting and developing team members
- Shaping a strategic vision
- Aligning others around a vision
- Staying on track
- Communicating with others in difficult circumstances
- Managing energy – yours and others'
- Dealing with life's storms
- How to enjoy your leadership journey
- Maximizing your learning from life's adventures

Read actively and take time to reflect on what the lessons mean for you in your particular life and leadership context. Reflection questions and suggested action steps are sprinkled through the book to help you do this. Don't try to do everything at once. Mountaineers get to the top with many small steps. Just pick a few actions at a time to work on and keep moving forward.

Whatever landscapes you find yourself in, I hope the stories you encounter along the way will help you find inspiration to be a more effective leader and increase your capacity to be a force for good in the world.

CHAPTER 1

Who Wants to Lead?

It was a stupid position to be in. I was off-route, about 140 feet above the ground, with no protection in place, on a climb several grades harder than I had ever done. Or at least, it seemed that way. My heart rate was elevated, and my palms were sweating. My belayer (safety-rope handler) was far below me and dizzy with the heat. Not that she could have helped much; I had been unable to place any protection, so if I fell, it would be all the way to the ground.

We were on the third day of a climbing trip near Courtright Reservoir in the Sierras. It was a scorcher, and the rock was hot, smooth, and slick with my perspiration. The cobalt blue waters of the lake beckoned in the distance.

Overconfidence and stubbornness had led me to push on far beyond the point of no return. I could have retreated in the first few feet of the climb, but a persistent streak, combined with a desire to impress my climbing partner, caused me to push on. Surely, I thought, there would be somewhere to insert some protection just a bit further up.

Friction climbs, like the one I was on, can be nerve-wracking because the lack of cracks and rock features makes it difficult to place any protection. They are notorious for long falls. Security lies in good balance, precise moves, and the friction from specialized climbing shoes. Sometimes, leading a business team can feel just as tenuous. How do we get ourselves in these positions?

When have you kept investing in a personal project or work project that you should have retreated from long ago?

As I clung to the rock, it seemed that the lesser of the two evils was to push on. I created fantasies of control. Climbing back down now would be much harder, and I would be even more likely to fall than if I kept pressing on. In my favor, I was moving well, and I was very fit. I was in my 20s, so I felt like I was invincible. Even if I did fall, I reasoned that I could stretch out and maximize the friction between my body and the rock as I fell. I imagined a dizzying but exhilarating slippery slide. If I did it right, I would be badly scraped up, but I at least I would not cartwheel out of control. The bottom 30 feet or so of the climb evened out in a slight angle, like a ramp, so I hoped I would slow down slightly before I launched into the river below.

Climbing stories are a bit like fishing stories about "the one that got away." I am sure some of them get wilder in our memories over the years. But it's often our perception of risks rather than the reality that shape our choices and behavior. What was the actual risk level in this case, though? The reality was that a fall from near the top of the climb would almost certainly have been fatal.

In life, we often badly underestimate or overestimate the risks and consequences of our actions because of the way our brains assess the risks and likelihood of specific events. We underestimate, for example, long-term health risks associated with poor nutritional or exercise choices because their impacts are not immediate. Some of us avoid travel because we overestimate the risks of spectacular events that are highlighted in the media – such as plane crashes. In business, once we make a decision, we are often overly optimistic about its success. We don't want to perceive ourselves as poor decision makers, so we interpret the data to match the reality we want to believe in.

Most occupations don't involve life-and-death choices like the one in the story above, but life offers, on a daily basis, conscious and unconscious choices to lead, follow, or simply not participate.

Who wants to lead? It is a question that often comes up when there are two equally capable climbers. And it is a key question to ask when determining who gets the next promotion or key assignment. Leadership is challenging enough without being on a climb you don't want to be on. Taking on a formal leadership role and title with the power to hire and fire, promote or punish, and praise or condemn is to assume additional power and responsibility.

In climbing, the distinctions between leading and following are clear. The risks, but also the adrenaline and satisfaction rewards, are far greater for the leader.

Followership

One of the things that enables leaders to have the courage to lead, though, is good followership. In climbing, the follower, or belayer, is responsible for taking in the excess rope as the leader climbs, which minimizes the distance the leader can fall. If followers take in the rope too tightly, though, they can pull a leader off the rock. It is a delicate dance of communication, coordination, and trust.

Is it possible for great leadership to exist in a vacuum without great followership?

While leaders are, by many definitions, out front, their power to achieve and drive change is multiplied greatly the more people they bring along, and the more inspired those followers are. Understanding the wants and needs of followers serves leaders greatly.

It may be a strange way to start a conversation about leadership, but I sometimes worry about the emphasis on leadership and the lack of discussion about good followership in workplaces.

In military college, one of the first things I learned was not leadership, but followership. I was given endless, ridiculous commands with the supposed intent of teaching what it was like to have to follow bad direction. From those orders, I learned team cohesion and alignment to values and standards even in the face of adversity or poor leadership. I also learned the difference between good and bad orders.

Aristotle said: "He who has never learned to obey cannot be a good commander." Great followers make great leaders.

Before you set out to lead, have you learned the lessons of good followership?

Good followership does not mean slavish obedience or losing your voice. It does mean honesty and speaking up courageously, diplomatically, and effectively when you believe a leader is wrong. It may also mean giving leaders the benefit of the doubt since they may be bound by confidentiality rules. Among other things, good followers bring a strong work ethic, demonstrate initiative in building their own capabilities, and support ethical values and practices of the organization through their words and actions.

Who Is the Real Leader?

While an insignia, title, or budget can tell you who holds authority, it can sometimes be hard to tell who the real leader is.

What does it mean for you to be a leader? Do you need a title, recognition, or compensation to be a leader? The answers to these questions will provide clues on what drives you as a leader.

In 2012, I reached the summit of Mount Everest. Though the glory on big mountaineering expeditions goes to the Westerners, it is in many ways the Sherpas who are the real leaders. We, the Western climbers, had individual responsibility for making many of the key choices on the mountain, such as when to turn back or when to push on to the next camp. Our decisions, though, were heavily weighted by the advice of the Sherpas. Not only did they know the mountain better, but they also had the extra energy reserves necessary for clear thinking. The Sherpas carried by far the heaviest loads, and they took the biggest physical risks in setting out the fixed lines that we followed and making more trips through the dangerous icefall sections. Sherpas exemplify the concept of great followership or servant leadership. They take tremendous pride in helping their clients to the top.

If you decide to lead, remember those who got you to the top. Is someone a leader if they have no followers? More than one military battle was lost because the leader failed to acknowledge excessive strain on support units, which then became unable to supply front-line troops effectively. Many a company reputation has been tarnished when growth in sales has exceeded the capacity for after-sales support.

Who is helping you get to the top? Are you doing enough to recognize their efforts?

Many organizations today value leadership above management. However, titled leadership roles come with additional administrative and management responsibilities. Many people find these tasks challenging, time-consuming, and draining if they do not see them as a complement to the leadership picture. Both management and leadership are needed. Management provides the efficiency and stability that gives leaders the luxury of planning ahead, which gives employees a sense of security.

How can your management and administrative tasks support your leadership vision and agenda? Avoid discounting the value of good management when you are talking up the need for leadership.

Transitions into formal leadership roles are often risky. Leaders transitioning into new roles fail during the first two years at rates of between 28 to 70%.[1] [2] Also, 35% to 90% of organizations fail to provide adequate support or training, making the transitions much more difficult for leaders.[3]

In considering when or whether you want to step into a formal leadership role, assess the level of organizational support as well as your readiness.

[1]   Lang, A. & Thomas, B. (n.d.). *Crossing the Canyon: From Technical Expert to First-Time Leader.* [PDF document]. Retrieved May 8, 2015, from http://www.ddiworld.com/DDI/media/articles/crossingthecanyon_ar_td.pdf?ext=.pdf

[2]   Bird, J. (2013, May 22). *Why 60% Of New Managers Fail.* Retrieved January 29, 2016, from http://internationalsuccessacademy.com/why-60-of-new-managers-fail/

[3]   D'Angelo, L. (2013, May 29). *Why first-time managers fail: How to avoid the no train wreck.* Retrieved January 29, 2016, from http://www.brw.com.au/p/leadership/why_first_time_managers_fail_how_JJst8pA6bk6Qi1jq20kb8I

Why Would You Want to Lead?

It's riskier, the workload is heavier, the expectations are greater, and you are under the microscope more as a leader. So why would you want to lead? Here are a few reasons:

Influence. Some leadership positions offer more opportunities to influence the direction of an organization. As a leader, you may get a broader view of the organization and insights into the long-term vision, which can be motivating. You may get the opportunity to propose and work on goals that are important to you.

Broader leadership scope also requires that you deal with the complexity of that broader view. You need to consider more stakeholders' views, and you need to address long-term planning. In hierarchical organizations, you have less opportunity to use direct leadership as you "climb the ladder," and you have to rely more on influence skills and, eventually, symbolic leadership.

Influence is not the same as control. While a leadership position may provide influence, many leaders note that they lost control as they progressed through their organizations. Some may enjoy those transitions; many prefer to stay within their areas of technical passion and expertise.

Which is your greater passion: to serve through direct application of your technical skills, or to promote a cause by seeking out greater influence?

Recognition. Recognition is another reason many people seek out visible leadership roles (but they can't count on it). It usually comes with additional responsibility, status, and financial rewards, hopefully after a period of challenges and testing, not before. Don't assume these rewards are automatic. As with military battles, due to the fog of war, not all who are worthy are recognized. Recognition may also not come quickly enough for some. Nevertheless, recognition, status, and possible financial compensation for additional risk and effort can be great draws for both leaders and followers.

Are you happy to lead even if you don't get the recognition?

16

Personal development. Personal development is another reason you might seek out a leadership role. Some careers, leadership included, naturally highlight our strengths and weaknesses, beliefs, values, and priorities. Leadership is a great tumbler, and it is the rough and tumble of corporate life that polishes leaders. Confucius said: "A gem cannot be polished without friction, nor man perfected without trials." Take on a leadership role and you will discover many things about yourself and how you work with others – lessons not just for work, but also for life.

Developing others. Being a leader also offers the opportunity to serve by developing others through coaching, mentoring, succession planning, and other talent-management responsibilities. Many leaders, once they get into a leadership position, find great satisfaction in this role.

So why do you want to take the lead?

- Getting to set the direction in your part of the organization?
- Additional budget or authority to make things happen?
- Recognition or status?
- Financial rewards?
- Increased responsibility?
- The chance to make a difference?
- Service?
- Personal growth?

What will motivate you through the challenges you will inevitably face as a leader?

Do I Have What It Takes?

In workshops to prepare individual contributors for leadership roles, participants often seem to ask: "Do I have what it takes to be a leader?" or "Am I ready to take the next step?" These questions are connected to how organizations define leadership and how individuals think they measure up against that standard. Corporations seek people to take on the management tasks associated with a leadership title and for someone to be the decision maker. Expectations on leaders are only increasing. Leaders are expected to:

- Be visionary while not taking their eyes off the details
- Be brilliant decision makers
- Stay abreast of industry changes
- Attend to an increasing number of managerial tasks
- Develop employees increasingly starved for development
- Be able to motivate people
- And more, all with fewer resources, less time, and tighter budgets

Organizations are still, far too often, looking for individual heroes rather than creating systems of leadership and distributing leadership tasks more broadly. They do themselves a disservice by publishing excessively long lists of the qualities they believe employees must have to be leaders, regardless of whether those qualities are truly necessary.

There are relatively few qualities that make leaders successful in all situations, and attempting to copy someone else's leadership persona can easily lead to a loss of authenticity.

For a week, I lived off the land in the Borneo jungle with a Penan native who is both an incredibly skilled bushman and a strong community leader. I ate eyeballs from wild pigs, fern tips, natural spinach, and other delicacies that we shot, trapped, or gathered from the forest. The Penan native's leadership capacity is based largely on his expertise in that landscape and his ability to maximize the resources in that setting. His way of life, though, is under threat from logging and palm oil plantations. Since leadership is situational, he won't have the same leadership capacity if he is forced to lead an urban lifestyle – unless he is able to identify and learn transferable skills.

What are the strengths you have that you can bring to different leadership roles and situations? Strengths Based Leadership *by Tom Rath and Barry Conchie is a great book to help you explore your transferable skills.*

Many leaders have been very successful despite their flaws. Leaders need, for example, to be able to build trust, energize people, maximize results, and model authenticity, but how they do that varies from leader to leader.

As long as it is legal, ethical, and not adversely impacting other aspects of the organization, allow diversity in approach, and help leaders build awareness of and manage their "allowable weaknesses." Emphasize what leaders can do rather than their traits.

As organizations become leaner yet simultaneously more complex, the list of expectations placed on the leaders only seems to grow. No wonder many people question whether they want to take on the title of leader. Leaders don't need to do it all themselves.

Create systems of leadership and communicate where you want others to step up rather than pile everything on a few individuals.

Can I Survive?

A question related to "Do I have what it takes to be a leader" is "Can I survive?" S'mores are a popular camping food in the U.S. You can check your likelihood of thriving as a leader in any situation by evaluating your performance with the SMORES formula:

Performance = Skill x Motivation x Opportunity x Resources x Energy x Self-awareness

Skills. Skills are a double-edged sword. They can help you, or they can get in your way. One of the toughest transitions for new leaders is the move from doing the work themselves to getting the work done through others. Leaders are rewarded for using their past skills, and they sometimes fail to recognize that a new job requires new skills, approaches, or competencies.

19

Accurate self-assessment of skills is important. Overconfidence (as in the earlier climbing story) can take you to places you shouldn't be or cause you to take things too casually when things go wrong.

Opportunity. Having leadership capacity is of no use if there are no opportunities to test or exercise it. Fortunately, there are many safe practice fields where you can try on the role. Volunteering for a local community agency, stepping in while the boss is away, or leading a project team are all small steps to taking on bigger responsibilities.

Resources. Resources can make a difference, but they may be less important than resourcefulness. While it is easier to lead a resourceful team, it does not build your leadership skills as quickly. For that reason, I am grateful for my early leadership experiences in nonprofit organizations. Working in nonprofit organizations promotes innovation and resourcefulness. You quickly discover the value of meaningful work as a driver of employee engagement when you don't have the option to offer large salaries and bonuses.

Energy. Your chances of thriving as a leader improve if you have energy reserves and you understand the interconnections between the types of energy. If you are struggling with your relationships at home, it might make sense to hold off on leading or let someone else lead for a while.

Self-awareness. Self-awareness helps you avoid your blind spots, leverage your strengths, and react more effectively to challenges. Do you demonstrate self-control when a series of big waves hit you, for example, when a big client leaves your account, followed by the second and third biggest accounts? Or do you transmit panic to your team?

Motivation. Motivation may be the most important of the elements. In the book *Deep Survival: Who Lives, Who Dies, and Why*, Laurence Gonzales investigates who survives in "avalanches, mountain accidents, [and amongst] sailors lost at sea...."[4] While you may never find yourself in these kinds of

---

4   Gonzales, L. (2003). *Deep Survival: Who Lives, Who Dies and Why*. New York, NY: W.W. Norton & Company.

situations, it is likely that you will find yourself fighting for your survival at some point in your career. Gonzales concludes: "It's not what's in your backpack that separates the quick from the dead. It's not even what's in your mind. […] It's what's in your heart."[5] In extended survival situations, having something to live for is a key survival factor.

If your only motivation for taking a leadership role is the extra money, you are probably more likely to surrender before things get too tough. You will give up when the cost-benefit equation gets out of balance or may endanger your career and the career wellbeing of those around you who may have to come to your rescue.

Service is a powerful motivation for many people. It implies a willingness to sacrifice one's career when necessary in order to achieve one's purpose. My brother's career involved some sacrifice, but he had some belated recognition. The following is an account in his words.

> When I was in the Western Australia Fisheries Department, I went through a traumatic process of closing a fishery to recreational and commercial fishing. It ended up saving a stock of fish from commercial, if not complete, extinction. It was traumatic because I became isolated from my department and everyone else, with both visible and real support diminishing as community support for the need to take action diminished. It ended up finishing my fisheries management career and is one of the reasons I moved to water resources.
>
> But 10 years later, the CEO of the Department of Fisheries called me to say that the department had just won the Premier's Prize for Public Sector Management for the recovery of the fish stock. He called me to thank me for what I had done 10 years previously to achieve this outcome. I was blown away. The key message is that it is never too late to recognize good work. For me, he showed incredible leadership – leadership that I have never seen anywhere else.

5   Ibid.

In many religions, work is a form of spiritual discipline, service, or servant leadership. On Mount Everest, I watched Sherpas carry the latrine drums back down the mountain as part of efforts to clean up campsites and provide a healthier expedition environment. In the Australian Army, officers don't eat until the troops are fed. During the Iditarod, an 1150-mile sled dog race held in temperatures down to wind-chill equivalents of minus 100 degrees Fahrenheit, mushers always eat after their dogs are fed. The 2014 winner crossed the line in eight days, 14 hours, and nine minutes. The musher Jeff King brought two of his hurting dogs into his sleeping bag to warm them up before he finally withdrew from the race to protect his team.

Loyalty and service cut both ways. The principle of leverage means that the most effective leaders get their results through the combined actions of their followers, not through their own actions. When employees know that their leaders care about them, not just the results, they are more engaged. Engaged employees contribute more discretionary effort, which in turn improves the long-term productivity and bottom line.

Apart from this utilitarian justification, accepting the rewards of leadership means you also accept the responsibility. Taking care of your people is the right thing to do. (If you would like to support development efforts in Nepal, check out these organizations: https://www.charitynavigator.org)

What opportunities do you have today to offer an act of service?

There are many ways to lead, both with and without a title, and many situations you can choose to lead in.

When asked about the top two reasons for taking the promotion, half of frontline leaders surveyed took the role because it would lead to great compensation—the number one reason for becoming a leader. What lagged behind? Broadening skills (39%), to advance their career (33%), making a greater contribution to the company (33%), and power and influence (21%). Surprisingly, wanting to lead others was almost at the bottom of the list of leaders' reasons, with only 23%.[6]

Some questions for reflection:

- *Do you want to lead? If so, in what ways?*
- *Why do you want to lead?*
- *How important is having the title?*
- *Are you willing to serve? If so, in what ways?*
- *How ready are you to lead? Check yourself with the SMORES formula.*
- *What do you have in your backpack? What skills and emotional and social resources do you have access to?*
- *What do you need to do to prepare to lead?*

Small steps

1. *Ask others questions such as "What is important to you?" and "How can I help?"*

2. *Review your actions weekly to see how you might serve first rather than expecting others to serve you.*

3. *Check out the website for the Greenleaf Center for Servant Leadership:* https://greenleaf.org/

4. *Join an organization where you can practice leading by being a servant to others.*

5. *List the transferable leadership skills that you have already gained from other life experiences.*

---

[6]   McCarthy, D. (2011, March 4). *Most New Managers Are Clueless About What It Takes to be Successful.* Retrieved May 8, 2015, from http://www.greatleadershipbydan.com/2011/03/most-new-managers-are-clueless-about.html

CHAPTER 2
Understanding the Landscape

Good strategies start with understanding the landscape you are operating in. This chapter explores how to read an organizational, social, or physical landscape. Reading a landscape correctly helps sharpen your strategic thinking.

The outdoors provides numerous metaphors to help you develop and refine strategy. How you approach a mountain, for example, can help you reflect on how you approach strategic goals. Most early big mountain expeditions copied siege tactics from the military by gradually building stockpiles of resources for a final push. Early Everest and African expeditions recruited hundreds of porters to shuttle supplies. Today, many of the very best climbers avoid that strategy in favor of a nimbler, faster, and lighter approach that leverages vastly improved technologies in weather forecasting, equipment, and communications.

The popular and contrasting stories of Scott and Amundsen, who raced to be the first to the South Pole are not just stories of different leadership styles. They are also stories of significant differences in capabilities for strategic planning and the impact these capabilities had on execution. In many ways, Scott was just as well resourced as Amundsen, but he was much less nimble because of the resources he selected and how he used them. Scott relied heavily on mechanical sledges, ponies, and man-hauling, which proved less reliable. Amundsen relied much more on dog-sled teams. Amundsen's team polished their skiing skills and were far more proficient than Scott's when man-hauling supplies. Although both Amundsen and Scott laid in depots of supplies, Amundsen's strategy was far nimbler and more flexible when faced with challenges such as extreme weather and poor snow conditions.

Some Definitions and Approaches to Strategy

[S]ome people believe that you must analyze the present carefully, anticipate changes in your market or industry, and, from this, plan how you'll succeed in the future. Meanwhile, others think that the future is just too difficult to predict, and they prefer to evolve their strategies organically.[7]

Whether the approach is planned, adaptive, or a combination of the two, strategy ideally:

[...] determines the direction and scope of an organization over the long term, and [...] it should determine how resources should be configured to meet the needs of markets and stakeholders.[8]

Another way to view strategy is that it is determining the approach to winning in a specific timeframe and situation.

What does winning mean for you, your team, or your organization? Is it a win if you conquer the mountain or gain the lead in market share but don't bring everyone back – or you never want to work together again?

If you want to win more than once or survive in the long term, adaptability in strategy and execution is key. Indra Nooyi, PepsiCo's CEO, commented: "we're all in the same business today—the business of adaptability. Failure to adapt can be fatal."[9]

Natural landscapes adapt and evolve over time; organizations have the same potential. Whether they evolve or not depends partly on the leadership's competency in three key areas: observing the landscape, interpreting the landscape, and intervening appropriately.[10]

---

7   The Mind Tools Editorial Team, (n.d.) *What is Strategy?* Retrieved January 20, 2015, from https://www.mindtools.com/pages/article/what-is-strategy.htm

8   Ibid.

9   Cobe, P. (2012, March 28). *For PepsiCo CEO Indra Nooyi, Adaptability is Key to Business Success.* Retrieved January 20, 2016, from http://www.restaurantbusinessonline.com/operations/leaders/pepsico-ceo-indra-nooyi-adaptability-key-business-success

10   Heifetz, R. A., Grashow, A., & Linsky, M. (2009). *The Practice of Adaptive Leadership: Tools and Tactics for Changing Your Organization and the World.* Cambridge, MA: Harvard Business Press.

To create more humane and profitable workplaces, it is insufficient to observe a system passively. We also need to interpret what is going on and then intervene effectively with leadership actions. Systems thinking and understanding the dynamism in systems are useful skills here.

Systems Thinking

"Systems thinking is a holistic approach to analysis that focuses on the way that a system's constituent parts interrelate and how systems work over time and within the context of larger systems."[11] The approach helps us recognize interdependencies, simplify complexities, design appropriate structures, and know when, where, and how to move through a landscape, or intervene to create a different result.

There are many kinds of systems, but common elements typically include:

- Boundaries in time and space
- Structure
- Subsystems
- Components or parts
- Relationships between the parts
- Processes
- Rules
- How the system behaves
- The purpose of the system

Below are a few examples of system behaviors and characteristics from the outdoors that have parallels in organizations.

What similar patterns are evident in your organization?

Dynamism. Landscapes, businesses, and other organizations are all dynamic. Understanding the patterns in a landscape's dynamism helps adventurers take advantage of opportunities and minimize threats since the same landscape can pose both risks and opportunities at different times.

---

[11] Rouse, M. (n.d.). *Systems thinking definition*. Retrieved January 20, 2015, from http:// searchcio.techtarget.com/definition/systems-thinking

Steep, hard snow poses more of a risk in falling, so you might think it is safer to wait until the snow softens up. But I have started climbs in Bolivia, New Zealand, Nepal, and Alaska as early as 8 p.m. to minimize the risks posed by collapsing snow bridges, avalanches, or falling ice cliffs, as these events tend to occur later in the day as the sun melts the snow.

Speed is one aspect of business strategies. Many mountaineers subscribe to the mantra that speed is safety since it leaves you less exposed to hazards such as the weather or avalanches. In business, speed to market or speed to volume can be a powerful competitive advantage. Sometimes, though, moving too quickly in a too-committed manner can lead to disaster. If a product is launched prematurely, it can damage a strong brand reputation. Knowing when to go fast and when to go slow requires a good understanding of the specific business landscape in which you are operating.

Patterns and cycles. The lower Deschutes River has some spectacular canyons and fun rafting rapids. The canyons funnel very challenging headwinds late in the afternoon, though. Knowing this pattern motivates rafters to get an early start. Retailers are trending towards earlier and earlier starts for sales around key holidays as they plan to take advantage of seasonal cycles. Investment companies try to predict bull and bear markets. Effective business leaders know the patterns and cycles that their industry goes through. Knowing these patterns and being able to leverage them is doubly powerful.

Knowing sales and other business cycles can also help you predict and ensure you are equipped to take advantage of rising market opportunities.

A whitewater rafting trip I led on the Shoalhaven River in Australia ended in a large expanse of flat water. We faced a long, exhausting paddle across the lake to reach our exit point, as rafts are not built for moving quickly over flat water. Shortly after we started, an unexpected tailwind blew up. We rigged improvised sails using tarps and paddles, saving us hours of paddling and energy.

Are you equipping your people with the knowledge, skills, and ability to adapt your strategy to the landscape and exploit opportunities as they arise? Discuss with them potential opportunities that may arise and under what conditions they have the authority to leverage resources to capitalize on them.

External forces. The variety of forces that drive human and physical systems to adapt partially explains why systems are so dynamic. Technology is one force.

The Bario Highlands used to be one of the most remote areas of Borneo. I drank rice wine with a long-house leader who could remember Australian and British commandos parachuting into the paddy fields during World War II to fight the Japanese. To him, the paratroopers looked like monkeys floating underneath pillows. The commandos had parachuted in because the first roads reached Bario only about eight years ago. Planes came slightly earlier but were unreliable, especially when massive thunderstorms would build up over the jungle in the afternoon, making flying dangerous. Until about 2010, people had to fly to the next big town to make a phone call. Today, though, a local award-winning development center is leveraging Internet technologies to train people in new occupations, allowing them to stay and work in the region rather than leaving for the bigger cities.

What is your team or organization doing to monitor transitions and changes in the landscape?

Some companies create a dashboard of qualitative and quantitative factors (economic, cultural, political, demographic, environmental, technological, etc.) that they track. This data can be gathered from stakeholder interviews, reports, think tanks, competitor analysis, site visits, etc. Once you have gathered the data, you can incorporate it into future scenario planning. Environmental scanning takes a broad view. You can then apply more detailed surveillance to factors you deem particularly relevant or intriguing.

Transition zones. Boundaries and transition zones are challenging places to live, but these are also areas of opportunity because fewer organisms and organizations are able to adapt to them successfully. Transition areas are inherently unstable and can be dangerous because of their shifting nature. They can be turbulent, dark, and disorienting. They are the places of maximum risks and opportunities, both in nature and in business. They can also be fun, as any surfer playing in the breaks at the edge of the ocean knows.

Transition zones in business often occur at the leading edge of new technologies, where new markets are emerging due to demographic or economic shifts, and as regulatory or compliance issues change. Examples include bio-printing, online education, social entrepreneurship, new battery technologies, and flexible electronics.

What are the critical transition zones in your organization? What opportunities might transitions open up for you as shifts occur?

Safe winter travel in Alaska requires an understanding of how to manage the transition zone between water and ice. While mountain biking on frozen rivers, I had to manage the risk of breaking through the ice. I could get swept under the ice and drown, or I could get soaked in the water, in which case I might be unable to light a fire and hypothermia would set in. The extreme cold meant I could quickly lose my fine motor skills. Traveling solo multiplied the risks. In some places, the river ice is very thick, and villagers use the river as a road. In other places, the river current erodes the underside of the ice while still leaving a thin layer deceptively intact. In training, I practiced reading the ice, cutting holes into the ice, jumping into the river, and climbing out and starting a fire as quickly as I could.

Know when and where the transition zones are for your organization. Create a system for capturing and sharing lessons learned from past transitions. What new capabilities or practices will you need to develop?

There are tactics for managing the increased risks inherent in transition zones. On thin ice, one strategy is to probe ahead. Businesses can probe ahead by using forecasting modeling, test markets, or pilot projects to avoid a risky all-in commitment. In crevassed terrain, skis can provide an extra measure of safety because they spread the load over a greater area. Companies can spread investments and risks in a new field by making small bets spread across a number of emerging technologies or players.

Provide effective training in change management so that people can move more smoothly through transitions. Anticipate likely scenarios and have effective crisis and transition management plans in place before you need them. (More on this later.)

Seeing patterns in chaos. Many people describe their workplaces as chaotic, but whitewater rafters and kayakers have long dealt with turbulent conditions. Kayakers read the river – they understand the patterns in the chaos, and they use their skills to take advantage of that apparent chaos, which enables them to negotiate the turbulence.

Are there underlying patterns in the chaos of your workflow that you can harness to your advantage? Are you equipping your organization to play in the chaos where others can only try to avoid it? Share industry and trend reports with your team to help them understand patterns in your business. Talk with industry old-timers to learn about trends over time. Build flexibility into your resourcing models to handle ups and downs.

As in business, being able to predict where changes occur on the river gives kayakers time to prepare. Rapids are formed in three ways: change in gradient, constrictions, and obstructions. In business, changes in gradient might equate to a new goal that precedes the ramping up of the production pace. Constrictions might equate to bottlenecks or limited resources spread across multiple priorities. Obstructions might include perceived logjams created by new regulations.

The following are some things kayakers look for.

What situations are equivalent in your organization?

Horizon lines: indicators that there is a vertical drop coming up. Approach with care. Send out scouts to bring information back to the team. Equivalent examples in business would be disruptive technologies, strategies, business models, or major legislative changes. Alibaba, one of the world's most valuable retailers, has no inventory. Facebook, the most popular media owner, creates no content. Apple and Google, the largest software owners, don't write any apps.

Chutes: deep green vees of water with minimal hazards. Enjoy the ride! Remember to celebrate and take note of what enabled that good period of performance so you can re-create it. These conditions often occur in the time between being the first to market after all the bugs have been worked out and before new competitors enter the market. Don't forget to look ahead; there's probably a new disruption coming soon.

Stoppers: rapids that get you stuck or can flip your boat. Go around them or punch hard through them if they are not too big. You might choose to overcome a competitor's new product by paddling harder with a larger sales force or offering short-term sales. On a personal leadership level, Lominger's 12 leadership competency framework lists 19 career stallers and stoppers that can disrupt or capsize a leader's career.

Eddies: a great place to pause and catch your breath while checking out what is coming up next. Most manufacturing companies have times in the calendar when production demands are slightly lower. Activities like strategic planning, external benchmarking, or training and development can be scheduled in advance during these slower periods.

---

[12]   Lombardo, M. M. & Eichinger, R. W. (2009). *FYI: For Your Improvement: A Guide for Development and Coaching.* Minneapolis, MN: Lominger International.

Kayakers build their skills at managing turbulence through skill camps, practice, and coaching. Provide employees with training in resilience and change management to successfully take on bigger and more frequent rapids.

> **Pendulum swings.** I was hanging upside down, suspended like a bat, high above New Zealand's Shotover River. Below me, the river rushed by. Beside me, a technician was nonchalantly chatting as he checked the rigging of my safety harness. Then, without warning, he pulled the pin. I flew face first towards the ground, and my heart leaped out of my chest. The river rushed up at me, and I felt a rapid, sharp stab of adrenaline flood into my system. Suddenly, the bungee caught me, and I waited for the upward rush of the bungee cord. Instead, I swung across the river in a huge arc, plunged downward again, and swung back to the other side.

One of the most common dynamics in business is the pendulum swing: periodic oscillations between priorities that are usually viewed as opposites. Common swings are centralization to decentralization, localization versus globalization, expansion and contraction, and regulation and deregulation. Some are the result of natural business cycles; others are the result of shifts in perspective or priority from key leaders. While some investors might want to take advantage of pendulum swings, most business owners will seek to stabilize conditions.

What are the most common pendulum swings in your organization? How can you build others' awareness and prepare them?

Kathy Long describes the approach of one financial service firm that had a great year in 2008 and a good year in 2009 when other companies in their sector were struggling to survive. On seeing the emerging trends, they simply called a meeting. The key was that they invited people with prior experience of the last big pendulum shift in the 80s and focused the meeting on what they had done to survive.[13]

It helps if you have retained people with organizational knowledge and if you value an organization's history.

Does your culture value historical lessons or simply regard the past as the past? Is your knowledge-management system set up to capture historical and anecdotal information?

Another key to addressing pendulum swings or polarities is to discard either/or thinking and view the polarities as "interdependent pairs of ideas that need each other over time to create and sustain success."[14] Linda Ray suggests: "when we leverage them both as a system, we are better able to achieve our goals."[15] Ray notes:

[I]n *Built to Last*, Jim Collins and Jerry Porras refer to polarity management as 'the genius of the "AND"', noting that it happened to be the distinguishing ingredient for companies that outperformed the stock market during the period of their research.[16]

Companies that do well over extended time periods don't just have excellent cultures – they have highly adaptable ones.

---

13   Long, K.A. (2010). The Next Pendulum Swing. *Business Rules Journal, 11*(3). Retrieved January 26, 2016, from http://www.brcommunity.com/b528.php

14   Ray, L. (2014, February 7). Managing Intractable Problems: The Neuroscience Of Polarity Thinking. [Web log post]. Retrieved January 20, 2015, from http://www.neuresourcegroup.com.au/managing-intractable-problems-the-neuroscience-of-polarity-thinking/

15   Ray, L. (2014, February 7). Managing Intractable Problems: The Neuroscience Of Polarity Thinking. [Web log post]. Retrieved January 20, 2015, from http://www.neuresourcegroup.com.au/managing-intractable-problems-the-neuroscience-of-polarity-thinking/

16   Ibid.

Interdependencies. One of my favorite ways to prepare for a big climb is trail running, especially through the magnificent redwood trees in California. I love to watch the mist rising and the sun filtering through the trees just after dawn. Ten minutes' drive from my house, there are trees that soar to 369 feet. The trails nearby have swooping banked curves and waterfalls that curl around the rocky creeks. The miles pass easily with such a beautiful backdrop. One of my favorite stretches of trail is a 13-mile downhill leg from Park Headquarters to the coast. It is a dizzying run along the edge of a bouncing redwood-lined creek that finishes at the ocean with a plunge into the Pacific breakers.

One day, I happened to glance at the root system of a large redwood that had blown over and saw something that surprised me. Instead of a deep taproot, these forest giants have a very shallow root system. When I spoke with a ranger later that day, I learned that the redwoods get their stability by interlacing their roots with the roots of their neighbors. Each tree holds its neighbors up.

Many of the commercial systems we operate in today are extremely complex and interconnected. When one part fails, it can bring down the whole system. The financial collapse of 2008 is a classic example.

How well do you and your employees understand the interdependencies within your business and between your business and key stakeholders? To minimize risks, examine who and what you are connected to and whether they are healthy and stable. If it falls, will it bring down your organization too?

Adaptive behaviors. One way to build adaptive capacity is to observe how animals and plants respond to opportunities, competition, and threats. Success in the wild is measured by survival and reproduction. Certain animals, like the coyote or fox, succeed by becoming opportunistic generalists. Some, such as ticks and leeches, succeed by becoming parasites. Moray eels and cleaner shrimp create symbiotic relationships. Echidnas and hedgehogs survive by narrow specialization. Each of these strategies has its risks. Specialization, for example, can help you find an area with no competition. However, it's a risky strategy if the landscape changes faster than you can adapt. Some examples could be deforestation or the introduction of a new, lower-priced competitor.

An ancient Greek parable states: "The fox knows many things, but the hedgehog knows one big thing." Foxes are highly successful in some environments, but they are less successful in other situations. In the article "The Hedgehog Concept: Using the Power of Simplicity to Succeed," they say the following about the parable:

> [T]he fox uses a variety of strategies to try to catch the hedgehog. It sneaks, pounces, races, and plays dead. And yet, every time, it walks away defeated, with a nose full of spines. The fox never learns that the hedgehog knows how to do one thing perfectly: defend itself.[17]

An individual or organization can find its specialization, its "Hedgehog Concept," by making three separate assessments:

1. Know what you or your people are passionate about

2. Identify what you are better at than anyone else

3. Determine your strengths in generating revenue.[18]

The path forward departs from where the three intersect. In the article I referred to previously, they provide this example:

> [I]magine that people in your organization are passionate about innovating, and about benefiting vulnerable people. You realize that you have the capability to be the best in the world at developing affordable water filtration systems and portable water carriers. You

---

17   The Mind Tools Editorial Team. (n.d.). *The Hedgehog Concept*. Retrieved January 20, 2015, from http://www.mindtools.com/pages/article/hedgehog-concept.htm

18   Ibid.

have a great charity network, and you have experience in making high-volume, major account sales.[19]

Tools that support the development of a Hedgehog Concept include values, mission and vision statements, SWOT analysis, Core Competency Analysis, a unique selling proposition, and competitor analysis.

Opportunities

All landscapes, business and natural, include a mixture of inherent risks and opportunities. The driest place on earth is the Atacama Desert in Chile, parts of which have shown no recordable precipitation for periods of eight to 10 years. I took a bus through this lunar landscape once, and for hours, I saw no vegetation whatsoever, just sand and rock. Water supply is a major challenge for towns on the edge of the desert. On the coast, however, there is persistent fog. Locals string fine mesh lines to catch droplets of water, which run into collecting vessels. They adapted this technique by observing the formation of early-morning dew on fishing lines that had been left out overnight.

Bio-inspiration, the practice of finding innovation in nature, is an emerging sub-field of innovation. The teddy bear cactus in Joshua Tree National Park looks cute and fuzzy, but if you touch it, the spines break off and hug you. The cactus became the genesis for a communications manager's plans to make corporate messages stickier. Redwood trees became the inspiration and logo for another group's renewed focus on efficiency and capturing ideas (coastal redwoods grow only along the West Coast fog belt, and their leaves have developed in a way that captures moisture from the fog, which maximizes a natural opportunity).

Use nature's examples as a stimulus for thinking about innovation. One bio-inspiration exercise is to send people out in pairs to sketch or photograph ways that nature is adapting to various challenges.

---

[19]   The Mind Tools Editorial Team. (n.d.). *The Hedgehog Concept.* Retrieved January 20, 2015, from http://www.mindtools.com/pages/article/hedgehog-concept.htm

Adaptability versus control. Western leadership models and literature concerning positive thinking have emphasized the exertion of personal will over others and the environment; "I am the master of my fate. I am the captain of my soul" (William Ernest Henley). Most people underestimate their capabilities, but issues that may be out of our control complicate real life. Timing plays a part in success or failure.

My first mountaineering partner ran for hours with 40 pounds of bricks in his backpack to train for big peaks. He had solid climbing experience and was superbly conditioned and well trained in avalanche prediction, avoidance, and survival. He was also the only person killed in a group of climbers that was hit by a massive "climax" avalanche in Nepal. Climax avalanches are the equivalent of black swan events in business – seemingly random and unpredictable with massive impacts. His group was camped on a ridge that they believed to be very secure and well out of the way of any known avalanche paths. But the avalanche that killed him started at the top of another ridge. It rolled down the side of that valley, climbed the slopes below their camp, steamrolled over it, and headed down towards base camp 3,000 feet below. In base camp, they wondered if the avalanche would hit them, but they managed to snap a few photos. I have seen those photos. No one who sees them can still believe that that we are complete masters of our fates. The only way to avoid that avalanche would have been if they had not been on the mountain.

Is your business positioned in the right location, or is it in the path of a strategic threat? How would you know?

There are ways to minimize the risk of being hit by an avalanche, just as there are ways to minimize the risk of industrial accidents. But sometimes, the sheer combination of forces makes them very unpredictable, and all we can do is put contingency plans in place and learn to adapt. Charles De Gaulle noted: "You have to be fast on your feet and adaptive or else a strategy is useless."

Stephen Covey, the author of *The 7 Habits of Highly Effective People: Restoring the Character Ethic*, popularized the concept of "Circles of Influence," which is a helpful tool for differentiating between when to control and when to adapt.

One useful activity is to have team members plot the factors impacting their world on a circles-of-influence chart. You can then facilitate a conversation about what they can do to let go of things outside of their control or where they should invest energy to shape and influence events.

One approach to building adaptability is to create a culture of learning. The longest surviving organizations are those that play, experiment, learn, and adapt.

In the winter months in New Zealand, you can often see keas sliding down the frozen roofs of mountain cabins. Keas are green, parrot-like birds, about the size of a chicken with sharp beaks and a mischievous nature. They are also playful learners and a dominant species in their ecosystem. They have destroyed many a pair of boots, backpacks, tires, windshield wipers, and tents.

Close to Christmas one year, I climbed Mount Aspiring, a beautiful soaring snow ridge in New Zealand's Southern Alps. While in base camp, I had taken the opportunity to write Christmas cards. I placed them in a stuff sack, closed it, and sealed the tent before we headed out to climb. Later, as I returned to camp, I followed a trail of cards across the snowfield back to the tent. A kea had ripped a hole in the tent, found the stuff sack, dragged it outside, and ripped it open. The wind had done the rest, carrying my Christmas cards downwind, scattering them along the glacier. You won't believe why you didn't get a Christmas card from me this year…

How well do you and your team combine learning and playing with ideas? Do you have a reliable process for scattering ideas around your organization?

One approach that worked well for me was to create a best-practices study team and report out on the latest learning approaches to the rest of the department. That pilot project worked well enough that the VP mandated replication of the process on other topics, and our team won a best practice award.

Tools for longevity. Survival rates for startups are poor, but even mature businesses can die prematurely. David Hanna researched companies with exceptional longevity and identified seven strategies to stay off the organizational endangered species list. They are:

1. Ecological Order: Strategize to fulfill the most important needs and expectations of your key stakeholders.

2. Purpose: Develop a compelling purpose and strategy so that each member instinctively acts to fulfill it.

3. Steady State: Design work processes that consistently deliver high-quality outputs.

4. Mobilization: Solve problems at their source.

5. Complexity: Build more self-sufficient, flexible, multi-skilled people and work units.

6. Synergy: Develop true partnerships with all stakeholders so that you always enjoy a competitive advantage.

7. Adaptation: Re-strategize and redeploy your resources in the midst of external changes to stay atop the lifecycle.[20]

Which of these strategies makes the most sense for your organization?

Scenario planning. Scenario planning is one tool that works well for promoting survival in both business and adventure environments. Here is one version and a few ways I used it in planning for my Everest expedition.

---

[20] Hanna, D.P. (2013). *The Organizational Survival Code.* Mapleton, UT: Hanaoka Publishing.

Define the problem/challenge/opportunity. Decide what you want to achieve, by when, and the time horizon you want to look at. Important factors to consider include a potential scope of plans and the range of scenarios you may encounter.

Example: I want to climb Mount Everest by one of the standard routes by age 55.

Gather data. Search for key factors, trends, uncertainties, and PESTs – political, economic, socio-cultural, and technological factors that might influence your plans. Examine any important assumptions you are making.

Example: I considered doing a traverse of Mount Everest from north to south, but the Chinese authorities were not granting permits for it the year I wanted to go.

Examine certainties and uncertainties. Examine trends and influencing factors from the perspective of how certain or uncertain they are, how controllable or uncontrollable they are, and how confident you are of your predictions. Sort the certainties in order of likelihood and/or favorability of outcomes.

Certain: I needed financial resources from some source.

Uncertain: The amount of money was within a broad but predictable band, depending on how many attempts I needed to summit, and what company I went with. The budget became more certain as planning progressed.

Develop scenarios. Create stories of the future around each of the certainties and the likely outcomes. Work down the list until the likelihood of a particular scenario does not seem worth considering.

Examples:

a. Warm temperatures and low snow led to increased rock fall and avalanche incidents in 2012, which led several guiding companies to cancel their expeditions.

b. I could get high altitude mountain sickness or pulmonary or cerebral edema. All three require descending from the mountain. The last two would mean canceling my efforts that season.

Use the scenarios in planning. I selected a company that had a track record of creating careful acclimatization plans. I had contingency funds for an ascent the following year so that I could minimize the pressure to push on if the safety risks were too high.

Use scenario analysis to help check assumptions and develop contingency plans.

Without challenging our assumptions, we tend to have a limited range of futures in mind. These are often overly optimistic.

If the new product launch fails, what will the impact be on the profit for that quarter? How will you replace the missing revenue? Check the range of scenarios you explore for contingency planning. Is the range wide enough? Use Schwartz's checklist for common types of scenarios:

- Evolution: All trends continue as expected. Things gently move toward a predictable end point.
- Revolution: A new factor fundamentally changes the situation.
- Cycles: What goes around comes around. Boom follows bust follows boom follows bust.
- Infinite Expansion: Exciting trends continue. Think of the computer industry in the 1950s.
- Lone Ranger: The triumph of the lone hero against the forces of inertia.
- My Generation: Changes in culture and demographics affect the situation.[21]

---

[21] Schwartz, P. (1991). *The Art of the Long View*. University of Michigan, MI: Doubleday.

Small Steps

1. *Apply strategic thinking to your life. Do a personal SWOT analysis: List your strengths, weaknesses, opportunities, or threats. Complete* Strengths Based Leadership *or similar tools for a general overview.*

2. *Practice your systems thinking skills. Spend some time in your garden or a local park. What niches exist in that ecosystem? How are plants and animals adapting to those niches? What can you learn from them?*

4. *Check what forecasting tools you have in place. Are they adequate for medium to long-range predictions of changes in the weather?*

5. *Invite customers to lunch and ask them how their world is changing. What will they want from you in the future to help them manage the impacts of those changes?*

CHAPTER 3

Where Are We Going?

"I chose the road less travelled. Now where the hell am I?"

– Unknown

Have you ever looked back at your life and wondered how you got there? Organizations frequently find themselves off track as well. It often starts with a lack of clarity about where they want to go – or failure to use tools to navigate and stay on track. This chapter looks at how we can build our capacity for vision and stay on track.

As in the outdoors, knowing where you have come from is often helpful. In business, it provides a reference point for maintaining organizational culture.

A good starting point for recreating an organization's historical path is to check the questions that you are asking. Ask the questions that a journalist would ask. The questions "Why?" and "Where?" are more strategic in nature; the questions "Who?" "When?" "Where?" "How?" and "How well? are more tactical.

Vision

Vision addresses the questions of where we are heading and why. This applies equally on the personal and organizational level. Without a personal or business vision, we are rudderless ships subject to the winds and tides. We jump from task to task or problem to problem, and in the fog, we lose sight of where we want to wind up.

Companies that enjoy enduring success have core values and a core purpose that remain fixed while their business strategies and practices endlessly adapt to a changing world.[22]

---

[22] Collins, J.C. & Porras, J.I. (1996, September). *Building Your Company's Vision*. Retrieved January 19, 2016, from https://hbr.org/1996/09/building-your-companys-vision

Create stability around "why" and flexibility around "how" and "when."

The challenge of preserving core capabilities while promoting adaptability and innovation is an ongoing balance between strategy and execution, however. How do we decide where we want to go? How do we keep our focus on the future? And how do we build capacity for vision in others and ourselves?

One starting point for shaping a personal or organizational vision is to understand ourselves and what we need in order to thrive rather than just survive. As Woodrow Wilson said:

> You are not here merely to make a living. You are here in order to enable the world to live more amply, with greater vision, with a finer spirit of hope and achievement. You are here to enrich the world, and you impoverish yourself if you forget the errand.[23]

Visionary leaders help us to heed this call, but we need to invest time to explore what that means for us. Leaders with clear personal vision and strong self-awareness can also support their organizations more effectively. Identity, whether it is personal or organizational, becomes part of the vision, but sometimes we lose our sense of identity. For example:

> [T]here was a time when Disney kind of lost its collective soul, in the early to mid-1980s when box office shares dwindled to less than 4%, and it turned down films like *Raiders of the Lost Ark* and *ET*—and was the target of investment raiders. Theme parks became real estate and their movies uninspired. Poor management was reflected in a poor understanding of vision and mission. Happy people were no longer center stage.[24]

---

[23]   Chapman, B. (2012, November 1). *Wilson's Wise Words*. Retrieved January 20, 2016, from http://www.trulyhumanleadership.com/?p=259

[24]   Rasmus, D.W. (2012, February 28). *Defining Your Company's Vision*. Retrieved January 19, 2016, from http://www.fastcompany.com/1821021/defining-your-companys-vision

Of course Disney, led by Walt, originally had a powerful identity of "making people happy." Disney's current mission is:

> [...] to be one of the world's leading producers and providers of entertainment and information. Using our portfolio of brands to differentiate our content, services and consumer products, we seek to develop the most creative, innovative and profitable entertainment experiences and related products in the world.[25]

One of these two vision statements is more engaging to employees and allows the company to flex and adapt more as the environment changes. The other answers more clearly the question of why the company exists and what it values rather than what it gains. One is outward focused; the other is inward focused. Vision and values go hand in hand and are key links in promoting employee engagement.

For new team members, one of the most pressing initial questions is "Why am I here?" Thoughts behind this question include: Is this organization, initiative, or project worth my time and emotional investment? Will I fit in? What can I contribute? Will my contributions be valued?

Help new team members answer these questions, and you will help them become productive much faster.

> A truly farsighted leader envisions a possible future that responds to and resonates with people's aspirations for their individual and collective success. When employees or potential employees hear about the good leader's vision, their visceral response is, *Yes, I want to go there too.*[26]

Does your vision pass this test?

---

25 Rasmus, D.W. (2012, February 28). *Defining Your Company's Vision*. Retrieved January 19, 2016, from http://www.fastcompany.com/1821021/defining-your-companys-vision

26 Andersen, E. (2012, November 21). *What Leading with Vision Really Means*. Retrieved January 19, 2016, from http://www.fastcompany.com/3003293/what-leading-vision-really-means

Setting Direction

In the winter of 1990, I set off down the frozen Yukon River on a 1500-mile trek from Dawson City in the interior of Canada to Nome on Alaska's Pacific Coast. It was a solo-mountain-bike trip, and I was towing a sled with my camping supplies and food. It was my attempt to retrace the route of the gold miners who had rushed between the dying Dawson City gold strikes to the new and promising strikes in Nome, where nuggets were "being plucked out of the sand" on the beaches. They traveled on bikes that were very heavy, very clunky, and very slow, and they wore fur hats and mittens for protection against the extreme cold. They had no fourth-generation super-wicking Capilene clothing, no anti-fog ski goggles, no rip-and-heat Mountain House meals. Instead, they had potluck meals, which probably consisted of muskrat, and they rested at warming cabins where they slept three-to-a-bunk after days of cycling in temperatures of minus 20–60 degrees Fahrenheit.

My trip was relatively comfortable compared to theirs, but it was still before the introduction of today's Fat Tire™ bikes. Instead, I welded together two wheel rims, ground out the join, and stretched a normal tire across the rims to get enough flotation on the snow. Because most of the huts are now gone, I carried up to 10 days' supplies. To tow my sled, I jury-rigged a flexible attachment to my bike seat using pieces of plastic plumbing pipe.

A maxim of survival when lost is to follow a river downstream to civilization. The Yukon is a very big river, however, and near Fort Yukon it braids out over the plains, creating a meandering maze of channels many miles wide. My maps were hopelessly out of date and at a scale that was nearly useless for detailed navigation.

Traveling through that maze, things seemed wrong. For one thing, the driftwood seemed to be lying at strange angles. I stopped and tried to understand what was going on. I observed the terrain and tried to calculate how far I had traveled and from where I had come. I looked for the sun, but in winter in Alaska, it's at that altitude when it's just a gray mush – not completely dark.

As I was pondering my situation, a small plane passed overhead. It banked and then circled back. I saw a small object fall from the plane – a message wrapped around a rock. The message read: "You're going the wrong way." Even though my task should have been simple – navigating down a river – I had nearly gotten lost. I was lucky to have someone overhead at just the right time to show me the right way and help me back on track.

The gold miners had a very clear sense of where they were headed and why. When employees are disengaged, it's harder for them to find meaning in their work. They might not see how their work aligns with the vision or see the leadership living the vision.

Even if your river seems wide and easy, it pays to check periodically where you are and where you are going. If you are leading others, you may think it's easy; just follow the river.

But do those behind you know which channel to take when confronted with a maze of choices or tasks to prioritize?

Be a pilot for them. You probably have a bigger view of things that will help them navigate. And throw them a message occasionally to help them stay on track.

Some tips for setting and clarifying a vision are:

- *Ask people periodically what they understand the vision of the company to be. Check for alignment of team members to verify that people are not drifting off track.*
- *Explain the context behind decisions so that people understand the why.*
- *Walk your talk. Seek feedback on how well your words and actions align with your vision and values.*
- *Share stories of people who model the spirit of the organization's vision.*
- *Anticipate how execution on the vision might change over time while keeping the values and spirit relatively stable. Sponsor a meeting that focuses only on creating scenarios of potential futures. Seek out thought leaders outside your group. Listen to renegades.*

Tools for navigation. Sometimes, the business landscape is wide open, and there may be many directions you can head in.

> Blue-water sailors have developed a range of tools to help them set direction rather than drift aimlessly in the sea of possibilities. Navigators from Micronesia regularly undertook sailing voyages of up to 2,000 miles across the Pacific in open canoes well before Europeans ventured forth. Suva's museum in Fiji has an amazing display of the navigational tools and techniques they used to stay on track before GPS, SatNav, sextants, or compasses were invented. Navigators wove sticks together to make star charts for sailing at night. They knew the bearings that marine phosphorous aligns along, and they knew how far from land each bird species would fly, giving them an estimate of the distance to land. Most amazing is how they knew the direction of islands from hundreds of miles away. The oldest, most experienced navigators hung their legs over the bow of the boat to sense the angle of the waves that had reflected off the land. Then they would give commands to keep the boat on track by reversing the bearing of the reflected wave's origins.

Speaking of origins, Adlai Stevenson has sage advice for those shaping the direction of an organization: "We can chart our future clearly and wisely only when we know the path which has led to the present."

In our desire to be innovators and future-focused leaders, we sometimes forget that our past can also serve as a navigation tool for the future. Howard Schultz noted: "When I returned as CEO in 2008, Starbucks had forgotten that meaningful innovations balance an organization's heritage with modern-day relevance and market differentiation, so we had to reorient."[27]

Alan Kay argues: "The best way to predict the future is to invent it." The world would look quite different without the innovative strengths of

---

[27] Advice from the Most Innovative Leaders. (n.d.). Retrieved January 20, 2016, from http://www.forbes.com/pictures/lmf45hfm/howard-schultz-starbucks/

leaders like Steve Jobs, Bill Gates, or Elon Musk. We tend to think of vision as strictly future-focused, but perhaps we should be looking 360 degrees like the Line Island navigators of old.

When leading change, explain how your new initiatives link back to the heritage vision rather than just serving as short-term commercial expedients. Invite the old-timers to retell stories of the original dream so that you can keep the vision alive. How might the values be honored in different ways in the future? Explore ways you can extend the vision sideways in interactions with suppliers and other key stakeholders.

Most companies have multiple metrics and tools that focus on what people need to do. It is less common to deploy tools to keep people on track with the long-term vision. Some tips for helping people stay on track with the vision are:

- *Hold feedback and performance management conversations that address how employees are contributing to the vision and values, not just completing tasks.*
- *Revise the reward system to reward not just what people do, but whether they do it in line with the vision and values.*
- *Link daily activities back to the vision when you assign tasks.*
- *Review task lists with less experienced employees to ensure they are focusing on the right activities.*
- *Create a "ladder board" of key team tasks to visually highlight the priorities. Talk about shifts in priorities and why those shifts are in line with the vision. Seek clarification upwards on those that aren't.*

Future focus. Part of the envisioning process is focusing on where you want to go. Athletes learn early on to anticipate where they want to be.

I learned this lesson the hard way kayaking on Class-III water on the Deschutes River. Class-III water is not usually life threatening, but it can contain some surprises and bounce you around, so it demands attention. John, my kayaking partner that day, and I, launched below a waterfall. We quickly hit some turbulent water, but it didn't seem too technically challenging. On a sunny day, few things are more fun than riding the waves, surfing the crests, and punching through small "stopper waves." Consequently, John, got a bit complacent, and suddenly, he found himself broadside to a stopper.

A stopper is like a vertical washing machine. They form when water plunges over a sudden drop. To get through stoppers, you need to punch through them with extra power and speed, or you risk getting "re-circulated" over and again. They can be very disorienting and sometimes quite dangerous. People drown every year in stoppers below dams and weirs.

John went over the stopper slightly sideways and far too slowly. I watched him get thrashed around several times and flushed out before he came upright in a shaky Eskimo roll. To keep an eye on John, I stopped paying attention to the currents beneath my boat. Before I knew it, I was going over the same stopper with very similar results, except that my spray skirt popped, and I was unable to roll the kayak. I was thrashed around, disoriented and confusedly searching for air as I was swept downstream, upside down. I bailed from the boat, took a 200-meter swim and got bounced repeatedly and painfully off the river bottom. I had been too busy watching what was happening immediately in front of me, and I had lost my future focus.

Business support functions are especially vulnerable to getting caught in near-term focus. Performance on immediate tasks is important for support functions to build credibility. But if they don't build a future picture, they are likely to remain as a pair of hands. In that role, you are constantly reacting to the rapids rather than anticipating and positioning the boat correctly.

Make sure someone has the task of looking downriver and planning the future so that everyone else is not constantly reacting to it.

Focus on what you want, not what you don't want. A variation of future focus is focusing on what you do want, not what you do not want. As organizations mature, they invariably seem to generate more policies and rules. These policies and rules almost always emphasize what the organization does not want, rather than what it does want.

Conduct a periodic pruning of rules and policies to weed out those that are no longer relevant, but before you do, make sure you understand why they were originally introduced. Counter the rule-creation trend by investing more time in reinforcing the values, behaviors, and culture you do want.

The militaries of NATO, Australia, New Zealand, and the U.S. employ a concept called "Commander's Intent" to enable troops to stay on track even in the fog of war. The Commanders Intent, a key part of a mission briefing, is a statement of the rationale for the overall objective, the *why* for the mission. If communication breaks down in the heat of battle or the leadership hierarchy is killed, the remaining troops remain aligned to the overall vision, have the appropriate motivation, and are able to move forward with the execution. This simple enabling tool provides more operational flexibility and agility.

Question your employees periodically to test their understanding of their Commander's Intent, not just their immediate tasks.

During my first week at the military academy, I learned that providing a clear vision of the goal while minimizing constraints in the method or process helps unlock creative problem solving. Sometimes the solution is in plain sight. The other cadets and I were exhausted after a day of slogging through the bush and running ambush drills, so we looked forward to relaxing for a few hours under our shelters, even on the bare ground. But after dark, we were ordered to "cammo up" again in field gear for another activity. (cont'd)

This turned out to be a military version of Storm the Lantern. Several senior classmen acting as DS (directing staff) were in a roped-off circle (the headquarters or HQ) about 15 feet in diameter. Their colleagues (sweepers), equipped with flashlights, were free to move through the bush outside the circle, but they could only do so as directed by their colleagues back in HQ. And the DS could only direct their colleagues to move when they detected one of us moving through the bush. They could not do random sweeps. Our task was to break into the HQ without being identified as intruders.

Most of the cadets viewed the activity as an exercise in stealth. I saw it differently. I lay low, hidden in some brush, for a considerable time, merely observing. I soon noticed that the dry leaves crackling underfoot made stealth extremely difficult, and my colleagues were quickly picked off one by one. So I stood up and started acting like one of the sweepers. I called out to HQ and gave them false directions, advancing towards the objective each time as flashlights probed in other directions. I worked my way up to HQ and walked in like I belonged there. I was the only cadet to reach the objective.

Tell people what you need to achieve and why, but give them as much flexibility as you can in how they achieve their goals.

Rules and constraints become prevalent partly because it is often easier to impose rules than do the hard work of engaging and aligning people to a common vision through dialogue. Roger Enrico, vice chairman of PepsiCo, argued: "The soft stuff is always harder than the hard stuff."

"Management by Objectives" (MBO) has a place, but the softer aspects of aligning values and vision rarely get the attention they deserve. MBO serves as a form of alignment but less commonly, engagement.

To improve alignment, ensure your employees understand why they are performing tasks, not just what they are expected to do. Revise reward and recognition systems to reinforce not just what people accomplish but also how they do it.

What Is Possible?

A benefit of understanding the landscape is that it often suggests a direction, opportunity, or possibility. Understanding the *why* behind a vision helps fuel people's passion for pushing through challenges or finding creative ways around obstacles. The explorers who became the most famous were those who had the biggest visions, explored the biggest landscapes, and were fueled by a compelling reason to keep going, even in the face of massive challenges. Many companies progressively decline because their vision is not big enough to inspire people to explore or push through the first barriers they encounter.

Isolation, hazards, and temperatures of minus 30 degrees Fahrenheit sorely tested my motivation for my 550-mile solo biking trip on the Yukon, but a clear rationale fueled my motivation. I wanted to see if I measured up, at least partially, to the early gold miners. As an outdoor instructor, I also wanted to re-experience what it was like for program participants to push themselves, and I wanted to build some professional credentials.

My "Wheels on the Ice" journey was inspired by James Mitchener's book *Alaska*. In this book, Mitchener describes a well-traveled trail that existed along the Yukon between 1900 and 1903 with warming huts every 20 to 25 miles. Most huts had fallen down long ago, but I was intrigued by the possibility of re-creating Mitchener's trip.

My first attempts at gathering information were not promising. Initially, the only map I had was a school atlas that seemed to show 200–300 mile, uninhabited stretches between towns. It seemed impossible. Apart from the dangers of riding solo for such long distances, there were logistical challenges like how to carry enough food and finding shoes that would work with bike pedals yet still keep my feet warm. (cont'd)

I was particularly taken aback when I spoke with some of the villagers in towns along the river over the phone. The first person I spoke with told me that five of his sons had drowned in the river after breaking through the ice while traveling on snow machines. Later, I visited a Spanish endurance team that had attempted to ski a part of the route. They had encountered minus-65-degree temperatures, and one of the team members was in the hospital recovering from surgery where they had amputated several of his frostbitten toes.

By taking it one step at a time, however, with better maps and local knowledge, a plan eventually emerged. I learned that the gaps between villages were smaller than I thought, so I could mail supplies ahead and plan on carrying only 10 days of food. I found some very warm boots that locals had developed. They were bulky but would work on top of my pedals and could also be used in a cross-country ski binding. I learned that the Yukon Quest dogsled race went along part of the route, promising a firmer trail for at least part of my expedition. My motivation built as I solved logistical problems and attracted support.

In today's fast-paced environment, you may have to set off with limited information and adjust along the way. Some tips that can help you get moving, then adjust are:

Pilot projects. Use pilot projects for learning and to test "proof of concept." An effective pilot project should include the following stages:

1. Plan and design the study (make sure you capture a baseline for performance before launching the pilot so you can verify improvement)

2. Change management training for key stakeholders

3. Support and monitor the study

4. Evaluate results

5. Make recommendations and improve[28]

---

[28] Kasunik, M. (2004) *Conducting Effective Pilot Studies*. [PDF file]. Retrieved January 20, 2016, from http://resources.sei.cmu.edu/asset_files/presentation/2004_017_001_22829.pdf

In the learning-and-development arena, change agents should test new-skill workshops on representative attendees, but first on a smaller audience. Seek feedback, learn fast, and modify the approach before a full-scale rollout. Beta testing with a sample of the intended audience is widely used in the IT field as the second phase of software testing.

Benchmarking. Benchmark outside your industry to see how other companies overcome challenges. Best practices in policies, processes and procedures, metrics, and standards are common areas of focus for benchmarking efforts. Benchmarking will work most optimally when best practices are adapted to your culture rather than just copied and pasted. Distinguish between best practice and common practice. Try to identify the factors that differentiate excellent individuals, teams, or organizations from average or below performers, since many practices will be common to both. Benchmarking can also stifle breakthrough thinking, since it looks at what is currently being achieved rather than what is truly possible.

Possibility thinking. Foster possibility thinking with the understanding that people will have the opportunity to test feasibility later. Read biographies of people who have pushed the boundaries of what is possible. How did they do it? Elon Musk, (PayPal, Tesla, SpaceX) for example, places great emphasis on "first principles" and challenging assumptions. Ask people to share their stories of personal challenges they have overcome and how they did that. Ask what it would it take to do something rather than if it could be done.

Seeking out local experts. Seeking out local experts rather than relying solely on documented information helps build relationships and captures information you might otherwise miss. You can't easily transfer implied information between people simply by writing it down. That information may be embedded in historical, cultural, or relational contexts in nuances related to values, priorities, or judgments. An astute interviewer might uncover some of this in interviews, but it is often more easily and efficiently transmitted through learning formats such as mentoring, coaching, communities of practice, or mastermind groups. Building these person-to-person learning platforms also strengthens relationships. Local experts can serve as guides to orient you to the mass of information available on many topics today.

Mind mapping. Create a mind map to build momentum and an understanding of your knowledge base and to identify skill and knowledge gaps. Once you know the blank spaces on your map, you can create plans to learn about those areas, building momentum as the blank spaces shrink. (On my Yukon expedition, the blank spaces between huts shrank from 300 to 30 miles). The mind-mapping process can be done either face to face or using software and sharing platforms. Both approaches work well for promoting collaboration.

Capacity for Vision

Our capacity for vision limits how far we can go. I nearly missed an amazing exploration opportunity once because of the limited range of my flashlight.

Tasmania, Australia, has some fantastic caving. Shortly after moving there, I found myself walking with some local speleologists along a limestone outcropping in a mountain ash forest, searching for undiscovered caves. The mountain ash is one of the tallest trees in the world, and some of the remaining original growth trees are massive in diameter. Slogging through the forest in the mud and rain, I had my head down. As I walked around one of the big trees, I nearly fell off a 150-foot cliff, which was the edge of a collapsed cave entrance that stretched approximately 120 feet across. I called the others over as I stared down into the pit. Below us was another layer of the forest floor growing like something out of *The Lost World*. Although excited to investigate, we did not have rappelling gear with us, so we had to return the next weekend for further exploration. (cont'd)

The next weekend, we rappelled into the pit and started exploring the cave floor. I moved across a sloping gravel area in a dark corner but paused when my senses started sending me a vague message. I had knocked down some rocks, but instead of hearing them stop, I kept hearing echoes as they kept bouncing further and further downwards. I moved carefully up to the edge of another drop, but my flashlight beam petered out in the inky blackness. I had no way of knowing how far the vertical pitch extended or what the possibilities were for this cave system because of the limits of my vision. I did, however, understand that we had stumbled on a major opportunity.

Again, we did not feel we had adequate equipment to go further and returned the following weekend with more powerful lights. We lowered over the edge of a 220-foot drop. Later explorations revealed another 60-foot drop, and the cave is now known as one of the deepest in Australia.

How strong is your vision? How far into the darkness of the future can it penetrate? Do you need to recharge your batteries, spending some time thinking about what is possible?

In every group, there are some people who have a greater natural capacity than others for long-range thinking or seeing the bigger picture. Seek them out, but also create periodic team opportunities to think beyond day-to-day activities.

Field of View

There is also a link between vision and what we focus on. In choosing a headlamp for my Everest trip, I was torn between a lighter, more restricted model and a very powerful but heavier one. For safety reasons, much travel on mountaineering expeditions occurs at night. I wanted to see as much as I could even at night, so I chose the heavier one. It had settings for both broad and narrow beams, and long and short range. Strategy can be compared to the broad view, and execution or tactics can be compared to the narrow, detailed beam. The short-range, narrow beam of my flashlight lit up the rock and snow in great detail at my feet. It enhanced my sense of security and enabled me to execute each small step with greater confidence. Occasionally, I would switch to wide angle to get a general sense of progress and review the upcoming challenges but also to enjoy the scenery of the broader view.

Tunnel vision is a risk when you are climbing, especially when you are tired. Focusing only on what is right in front of you can leave you vulnerable to emerging environmental threats such as changing weather coming from behind. One of the tensions of leadership in organizations is what to focus on. Good execution and efficiency demand attention to detail, but you also need to know where you are heading and what is coming up. Most managers get sucked into the immediate and don't spend enough time on the long view.

Switch your view periodically, short to long range, narrow to wide.

How Do You Know When You Are There?

The Song Dynasty's military used compasses for navigation as early as 1040. While the compass is a wonderful tool for tracking a direction, it also has its limits. It can point you in a direction, but it can't tell you what direction you should head if you don't know where you want to go.

Sometimes, the vision for a project or business arises out of the early stages of scientific exploration or from curiosity about a need that is not being filled. John Speke did not discover the source of the Nile simply by following a compass bearing; he had to gather local knowledge to know what general direction to head in. Not everyone, though, is comfortable being an explorer and dealing with that ambiguity.

Use celebratory milestones to highlight small wins and build confidence.

Part of progress on big mountains is acclimatization, which can occur even while people are not moving forward.

Highlight milestones that recognize learning and adapting, not just activity.

Shaping a vision starts with understanding yourself, where you want to head, and why. Even if you are following someone else's vision, you have a unique set of experiences, perspectives, and skills that you bring. Selling a vision to people can motivate them, but engaging with them to co-create a vision reaps greater long-term rewards for both the individual and organization in terms of ownership, adoption, and engagement. Holding to a vision requires tools for navigation, discipline, and focus, which I will address in later chapters.

Small Steps

1. *Ask each of your team members separately where they think the company will be in five years and how it will look differently. Compare the differences.*

2. *Rather than asking about problems, ask what is going well that you want to continue, expand, or apply in different ways.*

3. *Walk your talk. Ask someone to hold you accountable to living out the vision.*

4. *Develop mechanisms such as brand statements or elevator pitches to explain to stakeholders how your group supports the organization's vision.*

5. *Use team meetings, feedback sessions, performance reviews, and bonuses to link activities to the vision on a regular basis.*

CHAPTER 4

Building a Team

"Remember upon the conduct of each depends the fate of all."

– Alexander the Great

Meru, the film I referred to in the Introduction, documents one of the most outstanding big-wall alpine climbs of all time. The film highlights adaptability and shows how even world-class climbers need to manage transitions in the landscape and their teams. New leaders and those transitioning to higher levels of the organization also need to navigate some critical transitions. Like in past attempts on Meru, learning curves can be steep, and many don't make the climb. Common transitions involve shifts from:

- Doing the work yourself to getting work done through others
- Being a peer to managing peers
- An old organizational culture to a new one
- Technical focus to management and leadership focus
- Driving execution to being an architect of alignment

Check that your leadership onboarding programs and processes help leaders manage psychological transitions, not just teach them new skills.

Sometimes leaders have the luxury of building a team from scratch. More often, they must work with the talent they inherit. Selection, inclusion, engagement, and development of team members are key elements of setting teams up for success, whether in the mountains or business.

Choosing Team Members

Having the right team members can make or break an adventure. In the outdoors, partners with mismatched skills, goals, or expectations are at risk of dissension, failure to achieve their goals, or a serious accident.

When you are excited to launch a project, it is easy to grab the first enthusiastic person who comes along so you can get started. It's when things get tough that you find out the wisdom of your choices. It doesn't mean you can't work with new people; that is part of the fun. Just make sure you clarify why you want to be in business together.

Who are you in business with – and why?

Adventures reveal character. They show who is in it for personal glory and who puts the team first. Competitive threats, disruptive technologies, and recessions reveal the character, creativity, capabilities, and priorities of teams and their leaders during corporate adventures and crisis.

One of the benefits of planning your own venture, whether business or personal, is that you have the luxury of deciding whom you want to invite onto the team.

It's amazing to me how little care many managers seem to place on selecting the right team members. I have sat with managers during selection and promotion interviews, and I have conducted my own. From these experiences, I have noticed a few common errors and have some suggestions.

Selection

Select team members not just based on their technical skills but also based on what they bring to the team in terms of values, character, and contributions.

A team's total performance is more than the sum of its individual contributions, just as a climbing anchor is stronger when designed as a system. Teams perform better when the managers consider how the team members' different non-technical strengths can support each other. Similarly, empowering leaders within the team not only affects task completion, but it also sends a highly visible message about what you value as a leader. A team full of stars can be appealing initially, but it can be quite difficult to manage. Read between the lines of some of the early expedition books, and you will uncover challenges introduced by egos that were as big as some of the mountains they were climbing.

Inclusion

Leadership success is not just about selecting the right people. Another determinant is bringing them on board smoothly.

A huge talent gap exists in the industry, but organizational systems and support for onboarding or transitioning leaders remain poor or nonexistent. Downsizing and the thinning of middle-management ranks have exacerbated this situation. The talent gap is especially apparent at the supervisor level. In a recent Accenture survey, 48% of senior executives ranked effective supervisors as the largest or second-to-largest need in business.[29]

Effective inclusion begins with a positive experience of coming on board, something that is far from guaranteed. Newly tasked leaders are often left to fumble their way through without managerial support, or even the office resources they need to help them be effective.

I once relocated to take on an individual contributor role at a large global technology firm. However, when someone else left, they placed me in a leadership role, and within three days of starting, I was in charge of a global, company-wide project. I understood the need, and the developmental benefits of stretch assignments, but it was a very stressful start.

Do you have an effective onboarding process in place? Do you have processes (not just HR processes) at the team level for helping new leaders get up to speed quickly?

The reasons for failing to include people can be subtle. Rafters and kayakers know it's important to understand what is going on below the surface as well as on top.

---

[29] Robbins, J. (2013, January 15). *Solving US Manufacturing's New Talent Challenge*. Retrieved January 21, 2016, from http://www.industryweek.com/recruiting-retention/solving-us-manufacturings-new-talent-challenge

Two other corporate facilitators and I were rafting the Rogue River with the C-level team from a public utility firm. The team was all comprised of men except for one woman, a recent joiner. After a lengthy search, she had been carefully brought on board to be their first female executive. The trip was billed as a reward for the team because it had been functioning well. And so it appeared initially.

Over the first few days, the group seemed to be enjoying each other's company. They worked well together in the big rapids, quickly creating a coordinated team that responded easily to the river's challenges. They seemed like a very close-knit team with a lot of respect for each other. All seemed tranquil except for the crashing rapids.

The Rogue River is rightfully designated as a wild and scenic river, alternating between languid pools and turbulent Class-IV and Class-V rapids. Deer and bighorn sheep come down from the steep sides of the canyon to drink. Bears swim across the river on occasions, searching for dying salmon that litter the gravel banks after spawning.

A favorite rapid of many rafters is the Coffee Pot, which extends for about a 100 yards through a very narrow constriction in the river. Most rafting teams can't get through the rapid without getting caught by the undercurrents and ricocheting off the walls. Slight ripples on the surface disguise a surprising amount of subsurface turbulence.

Teams can appear that way when you first meet them. They may be smooth on the surface, with polite interactions and smiles all around. It is particularly common during the honeymoon phase of team development when everyone is getting to know each other and is on their best behavior. Deeper issues only reveal themselves with more exploration.

On the third day, we sensed that there was something not quite right in their team. Apart from working with the team to review their overall (cont'd) performance, in the evening, we took the opportunity to chat with the team members one on one. We discovered that their only female executive was physically and emotionally preparing to jump ship. We believed that the rest of the team was genuine in their interest in recruiting more women to senior leadership positions, but they were oblivious to her impending departure. Another expensive executive search was looming.

We had something of a dilemma on our hands since the woman had asked us to keep her decision confidential. We were not willing to break that confidence, but we also wanted to find a way to help the team.

In subsequent conversations, we learned that she was about to leave because she felt like she was being left out of the key decisions. Most of the major decisions were being discussed on the golf course prior to a more formal decision-making process. (The guys regularly got together for nine rounds, but she did not play. Today things might be different with more women playing, but at that time, it was less common). Lacking a full understanding of what the men had previously discussed, she found herself in a less influential position, and she felt they were ignoring her expertise. The rest of the team came to formal decision-making meetings confident that they had considered all the significant issues.

We explored with her the risks and rewards of raising her concerns with the rest of the team and left the choice with her, but it was not until we were sitting around the fire on the last evening that she decided to do so. Her comments stunned the team.

The executive team, including the departing executive, asked us to facilitate a conversation for them. As a result, they agreed to some changes in how they work together, and the soon-to-depart executive stayed on. The CEO initiated a road trip to his regional offices to explore other issues in their culture hindering inclusion.

Companies often spend big dollars attracting the right people, only to struggle with creating an inclusive environment that maximizes their contributions. The cause is often some form of unconscious bias or exclusionary behavior similar to the scenario where decision making was tied to golfing outings. Some ways to address unconscious biases are:

- *Create a process to identify when and how people feel excluded.*
- *Promote inclusion as a tool for engagement and productivity, not just as an HR requirement.*
- *Take an assessment to test yourself for hidden biases: https://implicit.harvard.edu/implicit/*
- *To overcome biases due to mental laziness, use a step-by-step process for decision making to help employees become more deliberate.*
- *To overcome biases towards people who seem different, seek out common goals and look for similarities.*

Building Engagement

One of the first ways we connect with others is the greeting we use. Tashi Deley, the Tibetan greeting roughly translated, means "I honor the greatness in you." Contrast that greeting and mindset with the superficiality of the American "Hello" or "Good morning." It's an interesting divergence on how we approach others, the degree to which we seek to know others, and the potential we see in them. Compare it, for example, to the way we assess people in this country. We emphasize intelligence tests that measure mathematical and linguistics skills over emotional and social intelligence, which are the real indicators of success in business and often in life. It's a very cognitive and transactional approach compared to most of the world.

I once attended a community meeting on a Maori marae in advance of a wilderness program for youth at risk. The meeting lasted all night and into the next morning. In such meetings, everyone from the youngest to the oldest has the right to speak. No one interrupts the person who holds the talking stick, but the respect seems to be returned by not taking up unnecessary airtime.

68

You may not have the luxury of this much time, but the principle applies. Being heard, or at least having the opportunity to speak, and having others pay attention goes a long way in promoting inclusion and engagement. In our drive for efficiency and time management, we often drive out the spaces for people to engage with each other. Don't be so efficient that you become ineffective.

Keep some open spaces for people to listen, be heard, connect, and share. Create and reinforce helpful norms for how people communicate in meetings. Use an external facilitator for particularly contentious issues to promote a sense of fairness in decision making.

A big missed opportunity in many organizations is their failure to take advantage of the fresh perspectives of new hires. Most companies are simply focused on getting the new person up to speed and productive. Companies usually communicate a message of "Learn how we do things, then we will entertain your ideas." By the time the new employee has learned "how we do things here," though, they often have little desire to rock the boat. I call this "the antibody effect." Organisms of all types are wired to reject outsiders.

This played out vividly during the orientation session for my Ph.D. program. We all gathered outside around a single loop of rope and were simply tasked with observing what happened. The group's actions could be summarized as avoiding rocking the boat. As a new cohort group, most people seemed focused on getting along with each other – except for me. I was interested in stirring things up a bit to get more learning from the activity. I pulled hard in one direction, shifted direction, and then drove strongly towards the center of the circle. I could see alarm and anxiety creeping across people's faces. I was not doing anything physically unsafe, just not doing what everyone else was doing. The group started uniting against me and eventually started trying to wrap me up in the rope and immobilize me. Debrief of the activity was intriguing. For me, it was an interesting reflection of the interaction between difference and inclusion. I was surprised at the depth of emotion that it generated for some people. I had seen the activity simply as a dispassionate experiment in learning.

Organizations exert significant effort seeking innovation, but that effort is often made more difficult because new employees need to feel they have to fit in to be valued.

Create opportunities for new employees to share, in an ethical way, how things were done where they were previously and why. Ask new hires: Before you joined us, what three words would you have used to describe us? What did your old company see as our strengths and weaknesses?

Developing Individuals and Teams

Organizations often choose to buy talent rather than build it because they are unaware of the talent they already have. Sometimes, talent only needs the right conditions to burst forth.

Deserts are often seen as barren and empty, but that denies the amazing potential for life that explodes there under the right conditions. I worked in the Joshua National Park during a seven-year drought for four years as an outdoor education instructor. It seemed like everything was focused on conserving resources and doing the minimum to survive – just like some corporate environments I have seen. Plants and people hunker down, don't share, and turn their leaves inward to hide from the harsh sun.

In my final year, though, we had an unusually wet winter that broke the drought. The result was an amazing kaleidoscope of colors that exploded across the landscape. Valleys of sand, gravel, and scrappy bushes became acres of purple flowers, which abutted acres of yellow petals lined up next to acres of mixed colors of all varieties. On the hillsides, shriveled barrel cacti became vibrant green cylinders covered in brilliant red blooms. I counted 36 on one barrel. Millions of dormant seeds had exploded into color after the rains and spring's warming sun.

Employees can also suddenly bloom when placed in the right conditions. Sometimes it's a job that is a better fit, sometimes it's a different approach from their leader, and sometimes it's a little extra coaching. Most organizations claim that people are their biggest asset. On the books, however, training and development are still generally recorded as an expense, not as an investment in the future of the company. The approach to HR is more often extractive like mining rather than farming where seeds planted today become the fruits of technical and leadership succession for the future. Companies would save a lot of the money on consultants' fees if they listened more carefully to their people and uncovered their buried talent.

Are you a leader who cultivates or extracts? Take a StrengthsFinder test, individually or with your team, to find talents that may be dormant. Ask your people what they most need to thrive. If you don't have time to develop people (although that should be a top priority), have competent team members coach or mentor each other. Research on mentoring suggests that the mentor often learns as much, if not more, than the mentee.

Recognize and harness teachable moments.

A teachable moment is the time at which learning a particular concept, principle, or skill becomes possible or easiest.

One teachable moment played out clearly at the Cheese Grater, a nasty rapid on the Deschutes River. At the Cheese Grater, the river runs over particularly rough rocks with just a little water to float boats. Just above the rapid is a narrow, tricky chute that often spits out rafters just in time for them to be grated.

My colleagues and I often served double duty as raft guides and facilitators on corporate team development programs, and we frequently sought out teachable moments. We always stopped above the chute to plan our route through, show our rafters the consequences of a spill if they were not focused, and explain what to do in a worst-case scenario. As other boats came through, we stood on the riverbank wearing lifejackets with emergency throw bags clipped to them, ready for fast action if necessary.

(cont'd)

> The drunken boaters came ricocheting off the walls of the chute spilling beer cans, equipment, and three rafters into the water. Inevitably, the swimmers were grated over the rocks. Our team performed beautifully. They caught the swimmers' attention with loud calls, landed three pinpoint throws with the rescue bags right in front of the now seriously sober trio, and dragged them to shore.
>
> The lessons of reconnaissance, preparation, training, and teamwork were thoroughly solidified that day in one visceral, teachable moment. Emotion, potentially large consequences, and success make for effective learning.

Start a habit of looking for and capitalizing on teachable moments to help develop your team. Leverage moments of rich emotion to inspire learning in new directions.

Shaping Performance

Before the days of plastic injection-molded kayaks, we had to build fiberglass kayaks a layer at a time, shaping the boat against a mold of what we wanted the final boat to look like. It was hot, painstaking work involving cutting, gluing, and massaging fiberglass into shape. People are much more varied, but some of the same principles apply in helping people develop their own shape while still aligning with corporate values.

In the Cheese Grater incident, our team did not suddenly step up to such a high performance level. They had drilled, taken onboard feedback, and learned while we encouraged them.

Write a weekly goal to catch each of your team members doing things right. Let them know what you have seen. It will help them grow and stay motivated while learning.

What do you do if someone's performance is well below expectations? You need to address the errors, but you can still employ the principle of catching people doing things right by shaping. Recognize and positively

72

reward, even in a small way, actions an employee takes that move in the direction you want.

A near-perfect application of this principle took place in a university psychology class. After learning the shaping principle from their professor, the students decided to test it out on him. The professor normally delivered his lecture from behind the lectern. Each time he took a step away from the lectern towards the door, the students would look up and give him a positive reinforcement of some form. They would, for example, nod in agreement, give him an animated smile, or furiously scribble notes. If he moved back towards the lectern, the students looked away, yawned, or disengaged in some other way.

Over time, the professor gradually moved further and further away from the lectern. The students, positively reinforced by their success in shaping the professor's behavior, kept playing their part. By the end of the semester, the professor was delivering his lecture almost from the doorway. The professor was initially angry when he found out what had happened, but after cooling down, he awarded the whole class A's for their perfect application of the principle.

Who is one person with potential that would benefit from you encouraging their behavior in a positive direction? Are your actions reinforcing the right behaviors? How do you know?

Develop flexibility in your leadership style. One thing both climbers and leaders struggle with is how tightly to hold the rope. For climbers, the rope is the connection between the leader and followers. In business, the leader is often seen as controlling the fate of the followers through tools such as performance management, assignment of tasks, and promotions. Ideally, it's more of a collaborative relationship. Hopefully, leaders are assessed on how well they get the work done through others. If the leaders fail to develop the skills of the employees, they wind up carrying the employees – doing their work for them.

When belaying lead climbers, I can often read their mood, even if they are silent, by the way the rope pulls through my hands. The rhythm and pace of their movements convey signals of confidence, fear, or the challenges they are encountering.

Similarly, as a lead climber, I can often tell how much faith my belayers have in my climbing abilities or their belaying skills. New belayers, or those who think I may fall, often take in the rope too tightly, which makes movement more difficult and increases the likelihood that I will fall. Too much slack or too much time between take-ins, though, tells me that the belayer is too casual about their responsibilities to me, the leader.

If my followers are constantly slipping, pulling on the rope, fearful, or exhausted when they reach the top of a climb, I have not done my job as a leader. I have selected a climb (task) that is beyond their current skill, or I have allowed them to get off-route into more difficult terrain. I may have described the climb unclearly or with insufficient direction. Climbing is an exercise in situational leadership.

In their book *Management of Organizational Behavior: Utilizing Human Resources,* Paul Hersey and Ken Blanchard suggest that leaders adjust their leadership style according to both the skill and motivational level of the employee.[30] In both business and climbing, the motivation for an identical task or climb can vary. The skill required for a climb or task can also vary depending on the conditions.

One winter, I climbed to the top of a rock pillar in Joshua Tree with a small group of program participants. The climb required no ropes, just good scrambling technique. Once we were on the top, a snowstorm hit us. It made the rock quite slippery, so we had to rig safety lines to descend.

---

[30]   Hersey, P. & Blanchard, K. H. (1977). *Management of Organizational Behavior: Utilizing Human Resources.* (3rd ed.) Englewood Cliffs, NJ: Prentice Hall.

Some suggestions for building a flexible leadership style are:

- *If conditions change – if you are shortening the time, reducing resources, or dealing with different stakeholders – remember that the task has just changed.*
- *The Golden Rule – "Do unto others as they would do unto you" – offers incomplete advice. It speaks to principles of interaction like fairness, appreciation, and justice, not to the specific methods each person needs to receive to experience those things. Adjust your leadership accordingly.*
- *Use Hersey and Blanchard's framework to assess each of your team members on a specific task. Determine what leadership style you think you should use. Ask your team members to share their self-perceptions of their competency and motivation for the same task. Discuss any differences in perception and adjust your leadership style if necessary.*

Developing Flexibility in Your Team's Skills

Another powerful step you can take for your team is to help them identify transferable skills. On the TV show *Dude You're Screwed*, a team consisting of a former Navy SEAL, an Air Force escape and evasion instructor, a Green Beret, and a primitive survival expert take turns kidnapping one another and dropping their peers in remote wilderness environments such as the mountains of Iceland or the South American Jungle. They have 100 hours to reach civilization with minimal survival gear. It has some similarities to a course start activity that I've used with corporate employees.

Imagine that you, along with all your team members, have just been blindfolded while traveling on a bus heading into the desert. You are guided off the bus, walked blindfolded into the desert, and asked to take a seat in the sand. The sun is beating on one side of your face, but otherwise you have no clues to orient yourself. You don't know what the landscape looks like or what hazards you might encounter, but you know you and your colleagues need to survive in this landscape for the next 10 days. You only have the backpacks you arrived with and whatever talents your team members have.

My facilitator colleagues and I used this exercise to assist corporate employees in thinking about their strengths and how they can adapt to new situations. We asked the participants to reflect on the skills and capabilities they brought with them that might be transferable to the new landscape. Some competencies, such as dealing with ambiguity, apply across a wide spectrum of jobs.

Identifying transferable skills can be particularly valuable for people whose self-perception is getting in the way of improved performance or appropriate risk-taking. Veterans offer amazing skills, often tested under battlefield conditions, but sometimes they struggle with translating their skills and experiences into corporate speak.

Help employees strip away the jargon and focus on the underlying skills or tasks they have completed.

Someone who had extensive experience in planning and maintaining transport supply lines in the Army, for example, may have very relevant skills for supply chain management in a distribution company. (If you want to help our veterans, check out www.fallenheroesfund.org.) A parent who has planned multiple creative birthday parties for their kids may have developed some event planning skills.

Are there similar business scenarios (entry of a new competitor into the market, technology shifts, change in the regulatory environment) you could pose to your team to help them identify their transferable skills and help them manage future changes?

Building Confidence

Part of a leader's role in individual and team development is helping build confidence. Working with employees' self-perceptions is one way to do it. Caving is one effective activity for uncovering limiting self-perceptions. Combining darkness, tight spaces, and the unknown, caving tends to draw out different experiences from people than rafting, climbing, or rappelling.

Body image issues particularly come to the fore. Many people limit their attempts at physical challenges because of their body image. Plato's allegory of the cave is, among other things, a powerful story of bringing our shadows, the weaknesses holding us back, into the light. In Plato's allegory, people need to be called into the light in order to grow.

How often do you hear the phrase, "There is no way we can do that?" I have heard it frequently when people first see, via a dim flashlight, some of the twisting, constricted passages I point out as the way forward in caves. Nevertheless, it is incredible how much courage people can bring to bear when they are determined to get through something.

As part of the culmination of a five-day expedition through Joshua Tree National Park, my team development facilitator colleagues and I often invited participants into a multi-hour caving experience. Teams were typically exhausted after days of backpacking, rappelling, and climbing. They had been mentally and emotionally on edge, so when a last-minute, unexpected challenge was revealed, it tested people's emotional reserves and capability to dig deep, in the same way that unexpected workplace changes have a stronger impact than those that are foreseen.

On one occasion, we were deep in a passage when the experience triggered a strong claustrophobic reaction from one of the participants. Her breathing became rapid, and you could hear panic starting to rise in her voice. She claimed she was stuck. Eventually, with coaching from the team, she figured out the puzzle, however, and wriggled through.

When someone is trying to get through a tight spot, getting breathing under control is incredibly valuable. Breathing impacts both our physiology and psychology. Physical touch, even a hand extended through the passage, also helps by reassuring people that they are not alone. In high-stress situations, our vision tends to constrict, thereby limiting our options. Get those who are panicking to move their heads and look around for new possibilities. Caving is a three-dimensional jigsaw puzzle. Finding a way through depends on being able to visualize and then maneuver the body to match the situation. Hips, shoulders, and the head are the widest parts, so one needs to align them with the widest part of a constriction.

Help people identify not just the shape of the challenges they are facing but also the strengths they bring. Train your project leaders to anticipate constraints and adjust the plan. Use people outside of the problem to coach others through obstacles by asking questions or providing encouragement or a sense of perspective.

Continuing the metaphor, it's important not to simply pull people through as long as they can move themselves. Physically, it increases the risk of injury. Emotionally and psychologically, it leaves people feeling disempowered and without improving their skills for managing future challenges. One of the things I learned in Search and Rescue training is that if you can safely help people rescue themselves they recover more quickly. During corporate layoffs, for example, helping people find a measure of control helps them transition more effectively.

What does feeling stuck feel like for you? Is it an inability to think clearly, a physical sense of being trapped, or something else? What helps you get unstuck? Can you communicate that effectively to others?

The stuck team member was coping well with the experience when I got word that another person was stuck further on. Her voice was starting to convey similar signs of claustrophobia. When the second team member got claustrophobic, I was not able to reach her directly, but her colleagues followed a similar coaching routine and were able to talk her through.

What triggered the claustrophobia for these individuals? Medical forms ask for information about issues like claustrophobia. Both individuals had experienced it before, but it was many years ago, and they believed it was no longer relevant. The first person had been locked inside some hay bale

(cont'd)

tunnels as a child while playing with friends. The caving experience was the first similar experience to re-trigger those feelings of claustrophobia for her. The second person, again as a child, had been locked, for protection, in a trailer closet by her mother, just before a tornado hit and tumbled the trailer three times. It was the first time she had been re-triggered since the tornado event.

How open are people to sharing information with you that they might be uncomfortable with? How might your leadership style be impacted by key events in your past?

The experience in the cave turned out to be emotionally transformational for these individuals. It also generated a lot of compassion within the team and led to some very deep discussions about what was blocking the team, metaphorically, from moving forward.

How well do you understand your own or others' triggers for great performance or challenges? To maximize your results as a leader, invest time up front in team member selection, inclusion, building engagement, and team and individual development.

As a leader, you get results through the efforts of others. The sooner you can get others up to speed and reaching their maximum potential, the sooner you create a multiplier effect from your team's efforts.

Small Steps

1. *Consider when it is appropriate to work as a team, and if so, what kind of team. Most working groups can benefit from at least some team-like behaviors.*

2. *When selecting team members, ensure you are assessing character, not just competence.*

3. *Make employee development a priority. The principle of leverage means you will get far more accomplished working through others than by doing the work yourself.*

4. *In the long-term, more diverse teams outperform homogenous teams. Seek out and capitalize on diversity in skills, worldview, experience, and work styles.*

5. *Use a team development framework as a thinking tool to plan the next phase of the team's growth.*

CHAPTER 5

Aligning a Team

James Murphy, a former fighter pilot and author of *Flawless Execution*, defines alignment as the link between flawless individual execution and strategy. Murphy's consulting company is called Afterburner, which is an appropriate metaphor for an extra level of performance that an individual, team, or organization taps into when everyone and everything are aligned and performing collectively, not just individually.

Alignment is relevant when leading yourself, within or across teams, and up and down an organization. There is a collective heat that you get through alignment that is not present in uncoordinated, individual actions. Conversely, if you and the team are misaligned, it is harder to maintain the fire and motivation.

Synergies, efficiencies, and an increased sense of engagement from being part of something bigger are a few of the benefits of alignment. Alignment is a key foundation of teamwork. It helps put contentious internal dynamics into perspective, permits individuals with different strengths to contribute to a greater cause, and helps overcome potential individual weaknesses in the team. Aligned groups can take on bigger projects and opportunities than individuals. An old Ethiopian proverb says: "When spiderwebs unite, they can tie up a lion."

While I was biking down the Yukon, I saw a huge formation of Canada geese flying overhead. They can fly 71% further when they align and draft off of each other than when they fly alone. Canada geese also employ other tactics to maximize the value of alignment. The lead position in the flock is the most challenging because there the leader must cut through

(cont'd)

While I was biking down the Yukon, I saw a huge formation of Canada geese flying overhead. They can fly 71% further when they align and draft off of each other than when they fly alone. Canada geese also employ other tactics to maximize the value of alignment. The lead position in the flock is the most challenging because there the leader must cut through the air resistance, so geese rotate the leadership. The rotation enables the leader to rest and recover while another takes its place. The objective (fly south before winter) is important to their collective survival, but it doesn't mean that the geese neglect the needs of the individual. If one goose is sick or injured, several others will follow it to the ground until it recovers. Afterward, the small group drafts off each other to catch up to the main flock. The honking you hear is the following geese encouraging the leaders to keep up the pace. Don't forget to honk for your leaders!

Another reason for alignment is individual and collective survival. A classic *National Geographic* photo was taken upwards from the ocean bottom, capturing a viewfinder filled with a huge school of minnows. Menacing barracuda circle below the school, waiting for an opportunity to wreak havoc.

I watched this scenario play out in real life while diving in Borneo. As I drifted along a coral wall of kaleidoscopic colors, a huge school of silver fish on the surface glittered in the sunlight. Bigger fish skulked below, mostly content to drift in parallel with the school. Occasionally, the larger fish would rush to the surface, attempting to cut a smaller fish from the school. Or even more damaging, they would try to break into the middle of the school. In half a dozen rushes, the larger fish were unsuccessful. Somehow, the school had been able to anticipate their moves. Even more importantly, they were perfectly aligned in their response to the threat. They wheeled, swerved, and jinked with incredible precision as a single unit. Eventually, the bigger fish swam off, apparently in search of less aligned, easier prey.

Alignment has advantages, not just in efficiency from drafting but also in warding off competitive threats.

Is your organization able to respond to a threat in the same way as the fish? How is your organization coordinating action to respond to threats? Does your team react to protect the group, or does everyone scatter to protect themselves and their interests?

Tools to Support Alignment

There are many other tools and ways to align a team apart from the commonly used management-by-objectives approach, which focuses more on what to align rather the *why* of the vision. Examples include storyboarding a common future picture, vision, mission, strategy scenarios, values, operating principles, the creation of common mental models, processes, communication strategies, pacing, and promoting engagement.

These tools all point to Peter Senge's leadership principle of creating common mental models.[31] The trick is getting all these tools aligned!

To overcome the mechanical and cognitive emphasis of alignment, read and apply the concept of emotional attunement introduced by Annie McKee, Richard Boyatzis, and Fran Johnston in *Becoming a Resonant Leader: Develop Your Emotional Intelligence, Renew Your Relationships, Sustain Your Effectiveness.*[32] Emotional attunement emphasizes the role of emotional and social intelligence in team and organizational culture.

We will look at a few of these tools now and address others in later chapters.

Good herding. Sometimes sheep are smarter and more aligned than executives. (As we explore this metaphor, you may think that the sheep equate to employees. I do not intend to draw a negative association but

---

[31] Senge, P. M. (1990) *The Fifth Discipline: The Art & Practice of the Learning Organization.* New York, NY: Doubleday/Currency.

[32] McKee, A., Boyatzis, R. E., & Johnston, F. (2008). *Becoming a Resonant Leader: Develop Your Emotional Intelligence, Renew Your Relationships, Sustain Your Effectiveness.* Boston, MA: Harvard Business School Pub.

simply illustrate a dynamic between the leaders and the employees that exists at work. Nevertheless, if you often find yourself feeling like you are being herded without understanding why, you may want to ask more questions to get more context and understanding.)

I attended a weeklong leadership development program at a ranch on the picturesque shores of Lake Wanaka in New Zealand. As part of one evening's entertainment, the master of ceremonies (MC) asked the most senior leaders to come out into the paddock, which held 15 sheep and one sheep pen. The 10 executives who stepped out were very bright people representing the top leadership level in a global high-tech company. Collectively, they were responsible for over 55,000 employees. They made individual strategic and operational decisions worth billions of dollars. The rest of the audience watched from the bleachers.

The MC gave the executives a simple task: to herd as many sheep as they could into the pen. The whistle blew, and they scattered. Not the sheep, the executives. No discussion, no collaboration. Every executive picked out his own sheep ran at it and tried to force it into the pen. The sheep wheeled, pivoted, and made the executives run around like – well – like a bunch of scattered sheep. When an executive got tired, or a sheep got too far out of reach, the executives headed off in a different direction.

Later, I overheard comments about how the executives chase the latest goal or management fad just like they had chased the closest sheep. Mid-level and junior managers frequently comment on how disruptive it is when those above them shift focus, which changes the direction and priorities, while providing little advance notice to those responsible for the execution. Those executives may be shifting direction as a response to changes in the market, regulations, or competitor actions, but their failure to signal those shifts creates lots of frustration for those below them. Or when they do shift direction, they mandate the change downwards with insufficient consideration of what it will take for midlevel or junior-level leaders to execute on that change in direction. Often, the additional work is simply added to existing work, resulting in dilution of effort, loss of clarity in direction, disengagement, and burnout.

Why is it that one or two trained dogs can herd sheep so successfully when 10 powerful executives can't? I don't know much about sheepherding, but it appears that keeping the sheep aligned as one group makes the task simpler. Clear, early signals help the dogs respond to a central leader's direction. In the sheepherding exercise, there was not one leader; there were 10, and they all headed in different directions, each chasing their own goals.

Are the members of your leadership team aligned towards common goals or are they chasing their own targets? Do your communication strategies enable quick changes in direction, or do they take a long time to trickle down?

One sheep was finally herded into the pen, not by the executives, but by a junior manager. He had been invited to join the executives because the MC found out that he was from Australia and "should know something about sheep." I remember that exercise very well because I was that manager. It gave me quite some credibility for a while because I was the only person who had any success! I observed the executives' uncoordinated actions, their lack of teamwork, and their rapidly shifting focus. Trying to influence the leaders was a futile exercise in the time available, so I singled out one sheep, focused all my efforts on it, stuck with that one, and used my rugby skills to crash-tackle it. I dragged the sheep unceremoniously into the pen just before the final whistle blew.

Even so, it was not as good a performance as a sheepdog. By using GPS data, researchers have explored how a shepherd and one dog can herd large flocks of seemingly unruly sheep. Apparently, "sheepdogs are making the most of the 'selfish herd theory' [put something between the threat and you] to bring the animals close together and move them where they want."[33]

---

[33] Marshall, C. (2014, August 27). *'Two simple rules' explain sheepdog behaviour.* Retrieved January 21, 2016, from http://www.bbc.com/news/science-environment-28936251

Are there common threats your organization faces that you could use to promote collaboration and cohesion?

In the example above, the lack of leadership alignment negated any collective intelligence the leaders may have had. Too many unaligned voices just added to the chaos and confusion. Many companies have brilliant leaders at the head of their functions, but executive teams with the ability to work successfully across functions are rarer.

Check that your metrics are promoting alignment to overall company goals, not just supporting individual functions.

A metrics-based approach to alignment may create other unintended consequences.

The jungles of tropical North Queensland are, not surprisingly, extremely wet. Among the locals, the weather and their ability to cope with it is something of a point of pride. Several coastal towns vied for the honor of being the wettest town in Australia, averaging almost 12 feet per year. One year, the competitive spirit reached the local papers when it was discovered that the manager of the post office in one of the towns had been boosting the town's reputation as the wettest place in Australia by topping up the rain gauge.

Make sure your metrics support alignment in values, not just results.

Pacing. Another way to align is through pacing and stretch. On remote climbs in New Zealand, your rope team has to do the heavy work of breaking trail itself. It can be exhausting, especially late in the day when the sun is beating down on you in soft snow. There are no Sherpas and no long lines of other climbers to kick steps ahead of you. There is an expectation that whoever is leading not only breaks the trail but also spaces the steps so that others can follow them easily and reinforce them for those following behind. They must not be too close together or too far apart, otherwise those following either have to kick their own steps, or they will unintentionally break down the edges of the existing steps. Aligning steps may mean compromising to find a pace and stretch that works for everyone, but it saves energy and improves the climbing team's overall efficiency of movement.

When you're roped together, find a pace that works for everyone to prevent whipsawing and the irritation that results from people jerking you around. Rotate leadership roles to ensure that one person does not get burned out. It also builds and maintains empathy for those in both leadership and followership roles.

Focus. Focus also plays a part in alignment. It's linked to strategy since "The essence of strategy is choosing what not to do" (Michael Porter). Focus helps with simplicity and makes it easier to understand the vision, goals, and communication. Complexity of action is the enemy of simplicity. Too many separate, uncoordinated actions, or actions where employees can't see the connections, create divergence rather than alignment.

To improve focus, scan the organization vertically and horizontally to ensure actions stay aligned and prioritized with the overall vision, mission, or strategic goals.

"You've got to think about big things while you're doing small things, so that all the small things go in the right direction" (Alvin Toffler).

Many organizations have online performance systems that attempt to align goals and activities. Still, surprisingly few companies allow their employees to see how their goals align across the organization, or even vertically above their immediate manager's goals.

Unless there is a competitive advantage or legal or strategic reason not to do so, promote broad visibility into goals to aid with coordination, reduce overlap, and leverage any potential synergies across groups.

Preparing for turbulence. Even when organizations start off well, external forces, internal friction, and lack of teamwork can knock them out of alignment.

The Class-V Gauley River in West Virginia is a blast to run, but to do it safely the crew must be well aligned and highly engaged. A spill in the big-volume water there can mean long and potentially dangerous swims. When a whitewater rafting crew is aligned, it has extra power, even when getting pushed around by strong side currents and powerful eddies.

To maximize power and efficiency, there needs to be alignment, not just between the captain and crew, but also amongst the crew. When paddlers are out of sync, they can miss an important turn, putting the craft and crew at risk. Therefore, rafters use a variety of methods to get, and stay, aligned. The captain issues warning commands to prepare the crew for action. These are followed by very crisp execution commands to align on timing. The corporate equivalent would be ensuring that everyone gets key messages at the same time.

Invest time in getting your team aligned before kicking off key projects or changes. The added efficiency will conserve your team's energy, reduce the risk of missteps, increase morale, and make for a more responsive team in the event that you have to speed up, slow down, or change direction.

When rafting, the variety of commands is limited to prevent confusion while in the noise and swiftly changing conditions of rapids. Captains set the cadence for the paddling through the volume and urgency of their voice. One person at the bow is designated as the lead paddler. The person beside the lead paddler is responsible for ensuring their paddle enters the water at the same time as the lead. Paddlers behind the two people at the bow are responsible for staying in sync with the lead and ensuring that paddles do not clash, which causes loss of efficiency.

Ensure that your team has clearly defined roles and responsibilities, that communications are planned strategically, and that everyone knows the signals that would indicate a change in direction for the project. Make sure you have succession plans in place in case your captain goes overboard, or key personnel are seconded to other projects.

In reality, alignment in high-performing raft crews begins well before the first rapids. As guides, we used repetitive drills for changing direction, stopping, pulling the boat sideways, rescuing a boater swept overboard, a capsized raft, or taking command if the captain was bounced out of the raft. Prior to entering a rapid, I would outline the overall strategy and contingency plans in case the raft was knocked off alignment from the intended plan.

When leading project teams, incorporate contingency processes for staying aligned if parts of your plan are knocked off schedule.

Communication. Communication is a key tool for staying aligned. When the intent is building alignment, it is best to start conversations where you can reach an agreement and build momentum. Usually, this means starting with *why* rather than *how* or *when*. Once there is alignment and goodwill, you can move into debates over timing and methods. Know how you will communicate with each other and what values you will align with even in rough water. Practice those skills before you need them.

Keep central messages simple.

"Great leaders are almost always great simplifiers, who can cut through argument, debate, and doubt to offer a solution everybody can understand" (General Colin Powell).

The Leader's Part in Alignment

Because employees model and adapt their behaviors to perceived expectations of their managers, a great place to start thinking about alignment is personal alignment. An old Chinese proverb states: "Not the cry, but the flight of a wild duck, leads the flock to fly and follow."

How well are you aligning your words and actions?

One coach described his leadership responsibilities as: "getting all my players playing for the name on the front of the jersey, not the one on the back" (Unknown). Modeling provides a good foundation for alignment, but it is insufficient by itself. Employees also need to see that those modeling the desired values are rewarded.

Leaders are architects of alignment between elements of an organization. They design the framework and select the tools and processes that shape the goals, organizational structure, and value systems. They also supervise the construction and integration of those systems whether at the individual, team, or organizational level. When vision, values, processes, activities, and rewards are out of alignment, the whole house can be unstable.

Balancing the needs of the individual, task, and team.

John Adair's life and leadership experiences include service as an Arctic trawler deckhand, platoon commander in the Scots Guards, adjutant in a Bedouin regiment of the Arab Legion, Honorary Professor of Leadership at the China Executive Leadership Academy, and Chair of Leadership Studies at the United Nations System Staff College.[34] These experiences have shaped John's view of the role of leadership.

A significant challenge for managers is balancing and aligning potentially competing needs, especially in the area of resource allocation. John sees the task, individual, and group needs as the three primary areas leaders should focus on, but the focus is constantly shifting. We can choose to highlight the differences between the three needs and play zero-sum games, or we can invest our energy in trying to align them. Assigning tasks that leverage an individual's strengths, for example, has been shown to increase engagement, and it also supports task accomplishment.

Try pairing team members with differing skills so that they support each other and can assist with development. Promote team cohesion while supporting task accomplishment. Set them up for success with clear tasking expectations and tone setting.

---

[34]   John Adair - *Leadership & Management*. (n.d.). Retrieved January 21, 2016, from http://www.johnadair.co.uk/

Jill, a senior manager for a major Australian bank, describes the challenges of balancing and aligning Adair's three areas of focus (task needs, individual needs, and group needs). Here is the story in her words.

I led a work team of three other women in a company Trailwalker team through 100 kilometers of Sydney bush over 48 hours, something I had done, running, in under 17 hours. To help them achieve their goals, I agreed to walk it with the women, which was not something I had done before. Together we devised a plan and tried to agree on our key objective. Was it finishing as a team of four? Was it about how much money we raised for Oxfam Australia? We defined our top objective as finishing as a team of four regardless of time [defining the task]. How would our key objectives influence our decisions, actions, and compromises along the way if we encountered problems with lack of sleep, injuries, or motivation [balancing individual needs against task needs]?

Three of us were quite fit; one person was mentally tough but a little unfit. I believed she could finish, but I was concerned that she might slow down the rest of the team. We set a realistic goal of 28 hours, which meant an average pace of just below 4 kph.

One of the team members, Jane, started to struggle early on. Our stops at the CPs (checkpoints) drifted on longer than planned, but we let this go as we had agreed that we would do whatever it took to get all four of us across that finish line [meeting individual needs to support the task].

As we got into the night, Jane's pace slowed significantly, and the team began to show signs of fracturing. The other two team members stopped waiting for us and were just going ahead and waiting for us at the CP. Teams had to check in together, so there was nothing to be gained by going ahead except not waiting out on the course. I was OK with this and spoke to the other two about going ahead since I did not want their morale to sink. I opted to stay with Jane.

(cont'd)

I now realized our 28-hour goal was unrealistic; 33 hours was now more realistic. I shared this information with the team at a CP around 4 a.m. They were all in agreement that we would keep going and that Jane should not pull out, even though she was battling a bad cough (she would later be diagnosed with a chest infection) [the team's best intentions would be further tested].

At one point, our pace dropped to 2 kph, and the other two waited for us for an hour and a half at the next CP. By the second-to-last CP, I had been with Jane all through the night while the other two had pressed ahead. Neither Jane nor I had slept for 31 hours.

I now felt an overwhelming surge of guilt as the team leader. I realized that I had let the other two women down. I had focused all my effort and attention on helping Jane achieve her goal, knowing that the other two were at a different fitness level.

At the next CP, we all discussed Jane's condition. The other two wanted her to pull out, but I spoke up and said that she had gotten this far – 89 kilometers. There were only 11 kilometers to go. Were we entitled to ask her to pull out after coming so close? I understood that they both just wanted to finish the event, but I reminded them that our key objective had been the team and finishing together [balancing group and individual needs].

They reluctantly agreed. We also agreed that as Cliff, Jane's partner who had run up from the finish line, was happy to stay with Jane, the other three of us would go ahead and wait for her at the finish line where we would cross as a team [balancing individual, task and team needs]. Jane was OK with this arrangement. She even insisted on it, feeling that she had slowed down the team a lot. We crossed the finish line together and covered the 100 kilometers in just less than 36 hours. Although some individual preferences for a faster time were not met, the primary objective of completing the race [task] together [group] was met without serious injury to anyone [individual needs].

Some of the lessons inherent in Jill's story are:

Leaders need to be able to balance competing needs – getting the job (task) done, meeting individual needs and preferences, and creating and maintaining a positive team or group climate.

This balancing act can be emotionally draining for leaders. Leaders can also get hooked into the needs of an individual – potentially to the detriment of the team or task (the squeaky wheel gets the grease). Use Adair's framework to bring some objectivity. Which of the three needs is most important at this time?

When possible, a good place to invest your leadership time is in activities where all three needs intersect.

Remember, though, leaders don't need to meet all these needs themselves. There may, for example, be someone in your group who is great at organizing group get-togethers if you aren't inclined. Your job is to create the space and permission.

Look for synergies in meeting potentially conflicting needs. Has someone shown interest in learning a skill that would also help you meet task needs? Building skills at finding win-wins and assuming the best of others can help minimize conflicts arising from competing needs. Create a fair system ahead of time for resolving conflicting needs.

Small Steps

1. *Extend your own capacity for emotional and social intelligence. Take a self or 360-degree assessment, read some books on emotional intelligence, or take a workshop to get started.*

2. *Audit your organizational processes, such as performance management, talent management, resource allocation, and goal setting, to identify where they are misaligned with your values, vision, mission, or culture.*

3. *Prioritize your efforts on alignment. Do you want or need 100% alignment? Be careful that alignment does not become unthinking compliance and drive out appropriate dissent or innovation.*

4. *Consider different types of alignment. Many organizations still emphasize vertical alignment in their performance management systems, but the reality is that many work processes cut across departments and stakeholders. Ask your stakeholders where they feel out of alignment with you.*

5. *Help your team to ask why, not just what and when. Having meaningful work helps reinforce a sense of purpose and increases employee engagement.*

CHAPTER 6

Leading a Team

Is leadership an art or science? At the moment, it's still both. On my first attempt to climb Aconcagua, the highest point in South America at 22,841 feet, I was part of a very fit, well-motivated team that got along well. None of us reached the summit. On my second attempt, the team was much older, much less fit, and did not get along nearly as well. We all reached the top.

Why does one team fail while another succeeds in spite of fewer favorable conditions? This chapter looks at how to bring out the best in teams and how we view our role as leaders.

A Compelling Final Expedition

One of the most powerful examples of team leadership I've experienced occurred during a "Final Expedition" on a 10-day Outward Bound trip in Joshua Tree National Park. Joshua Tree is a wild landscape of winding canyons, sandstone tunnels, bizarre trees, and strange rock formations. The Final is a capstone experience in which participants select and execute their culminating expedition. The instructors shadow the group for safety but delegate most responsibilities to the team. This expedition is intended as proof that the participants are able to apply the skills they have progressively acquired during the program.

The group of 10, mostly beginners in the outdoors, gathered from around the country. They had been learning to climb, rappel, cave, navigate, and live successfully in a desert landscape. They had also learned techniques for managing their group dynamics including shaping a team climate, decision making, planning, and team leadership. They had learned very well.

(cont'd)

In fact, they had learned so well that when we outlined three options for a final expedition for them, we included an option that I had only offered once before in five years. This option was a very committing and strenuous route through a convoluted canyon system. It was long, but more significantly it provided serious navigation and safety issues. Boulders the size of houses lay stacked on top of each other at crazy angles, leaving underground tunnels and crazy drop-offs. The route was challenging enough on its own, but it was doubly difficult when carrying large packs. Once we dropped into the canyon, we would be committed and turning back would be extremely difficult.

If the group chose this option, they would need to continue making difficult judgments regarding safety and balancing individual and team needs while getting the job done. It would also be a highly stressful time for us, the instructors, since we would delegate responsibility for execution but remain accountable if anything went wrong. In the event of even a relatively minor accident like a twisted ankle, we would be forced into an emergency bivouac in the canyon. There was also the potential for a far more serious accident if everyone was not completely focused, and we made this very clear to the group. On the other hand, if they were successful, it would be a journey they would remember for the rest of their lives.

We sat down in a circle in a sandy wash, recapped the options, and proceeded to go around the circle talking about which of the three options people wanted to take. In increasing order of difficulty, the three options were:

1. An easy route following clear trails

2. A moderately difficult canyon route that involved some scrambling and pack passing around obstacles

3. The canyon described above

(cont'd)

The group was full of energy and rightfully confident in their skills, so it did not surprise me that one after the other voted to take the most challenging route – until it came to the last person. Her comments, paraphrased, were that she would be very happy to take the easiest route alone and wished them the best, but she could not, and would not, take the most challenging canyon descent.

Her words floored the group. The highlight of the trip, the culminating goal they had been working hard toward, was at risk. They were faced with someone who seemed very resolute but lacked confidence in her own skills. The group tried to throw the decision back to us, but we explained that the decision was now up to them. We reminded them that they had decision-making tools and that they had practiced for interpersonal challenges, not just physical ones.

What emerged was some of the most powerful emotional-intelligence work I have seen from any group, even among seasoned leaders, let alone a group that had known each other for just eight days and was in a largely unfamiliar environment.

The group stated, quite transparently, that they would be very disappointed (individual needs) if they could not do the most challenging option (task needs). However, almost the first thing they said was that they "started this together" and wanted to finish it together (group needs), even if they had to sacrifice their goal to allow her to participate (individual needs). In return, the group asked if she would be willing to help them understand her concerns and be open to them exploring ways to address her concerns. She allowed for such a conversation, and the group skillfully inquired about her challenges. Some of her concerns were that she would hold back the group and that she had a fear of heights (although she had been climbing and rappelling during the training phase of the expedition). She was also concerned about carrying heavy packs through unknown and more difficult terrain than they had experienced. The group listened with empathy and shared their concerns, but they also explored possible solutions (aligning task, group, and individual needs).

(cont'd)

Eventually, the conversation wound down. It was time for a decision. They offered her time to think further if she needed it. They were surprised when she said with a grim, determined face: "No, I've made my decision." The group's faces were crestfallen but then elated as she said: "Let's do it – but I will need your help."

Spirits were high as we approached the entrance to the canyon. Then, as we reached the rim of the canyon, reality set in. It was more intimidating than they had imagined. The most gung-ho, enthusiastic team members were the most awed, and we could see uncertainty settling in.

Because the terrain was very tricky, we shadowed the group closely enough to see and hear the conversations that were going on. We observed the changes in how the individuals and group were moving. The group was heading toward a motivational crisis point, and there was still the possibility of turning back, abandoning their goal, and taking the easy way out.

It was then that our previously reluctant participant stepped up in both a real and symbolic way. She picked up the largest pack and moved to the front of the stalled group, slapping people on the back, and offering words of encouragement as she went. She was now physically in the lead, and as the rest of the group saw how she pushed through her fears, she inspired them. She became the informal leader of that group.

I will always remember that group as one of the most time efficient, effective, and caring groups I have seen. They moved through that canyon not only most quickly but also most safely. They were consistently looking out for each other, anticipating the next tricky move around a boulder, checking in with each other, and backing up each other. It was a truly integrated team in which people operated effectively as individuals, in subgroups, and as a whole unit. The celebration at the end of the canyon was not just one of achievement but also one of camaraderie and reflection on where they had started as a team and where they had ended up.

Important elements of team leadership as illustrated in the Final Expedition. Teams work best when they have sufficient authority, resources, competence, and access to get the job done, and effective team leadership that pays attention to the following:

Common goals. The team created a strong track record of goal accomplishment over 10 days, and they strove for clarity of common goals. They demonstrated an ability to integrate individual goals in pursuit of team goals, and they generated individual commitment and encouraged cooperation towards those common goals.

A strategic planning process. Like other healthy teams, they showed a collective vision and direction tied to a clear overall purpose. While some of their objectives revolved around the achievement of accomplishments, the team's highest stated purpose was to "learn and model as much as they could about great leadership" through their learning experiences.

Shared values and ethics. The group demonstrated well-established values and ethics during their decision-making process and the way they treated each other. They modeled ethical courage in sticking to their highest values when faced with the challenge of potentially competing individual goals.

Customer focus. Strong teams have a clear understanding of their key customers' internal and external needs. In this case, the customers were internal, and they developed a strong understanding of each other's needs through thoughtful questioning, careful listening, and demonstrating respect. They strove for a win-win to align everyone's needs.

Common processes and problem-solving and decision-making tools. Effective teams utilize structured collaboration processes to define problems and create and implement alternative solutions. The team used a variety of problem-solving techniques that they had previously practiced, including a seven-step problem-solving framework, a round-robin process to get all opinions out, and a conflict resolution framework.

Open and clear communication. Clearly evident in the curiosity, thoughtful questioning, and attentive listening, this team clearly demonstrated appropriate mutual sharing, honesty, courageous conversations, and striving for clarity, which are all indicators of a team that understands how to communicate effectively with each other. Business teams would also want to exhibit these qualities in communication with other stakeholders such as customers, suppliers, other departments, or regulators.

An effective on-boarding process. "An effective onboarding process usually includes team roles, team values, team operating principles, strategic aspects of the team, communications and clarification of performance expectations."[35] In this case, the facilitators had been responsible for their onboarding, but the team carried forward the principles and practices into the Final Expedition.

Task Planning. The team utilized processes for determining and allocating tasks such as navigation, safety management, and distributing loads. Effective teams address issues such as resource allocation, prioritization, roles, and skill allocation, all of which they did. By addressing these items, they created the conditions for some exceptional individual leadership to emerge. Trust between team members, effective leadership, high morale, and high task accomplishment are the result of leaders and team members successfully addressing these items.

When have you seen teams operate at their best? What was your contribution? How can you re-create conditions likely to increase the chances of high performance recurring?

The Leader's Role

It can be easy to get lost in the maze of tasks that you are expected to take on as a manager.

To simplify and align expectations, consider the role, or roles, that you want to take on as a leader.

---

[35]　Emelo, R. & Reed, T. (1999). *Dynamics of Team Performance.* (Facilitators Training Manual). (4th ed.) Cincinnati, Ohio: Triple Creek Associates.

The agenda that you shape for yourself and how you prioritize tasks is likely to be shaped by how you perceive your role. There are many metaphors that have been used to describe the role of a leader. Let's explore a few that the outdoors might bring to mind.

The leader as navigator. Max De Pree, CEO of Herman Miller, a furniture company lauded for its inclusive and caring culture, suggested: "The first responsibility of a leader is to define reality." With all the information that is available today, we don't have so much a content-communication problem as much as we have a context problem. Leaders, with their wider access to information, can fill valuable roles as map-readers and interpreters of the landscape.

A map is a representation of the territory. It's not the actual territory, but it helps us navigate. It reduces complexity, provides a sense of scale and direction, and identifies important features of the terrain. It also notes unique attributes, hazards, and opportunities inherent in the landscape.

I have misread the map more than once in the outdoors. It's embarrassing and potentially dangerous. If you often misread the map in business, it can undercut your credibility. You don't have to be the sole map-reader.

To avoid navigational errors when executing plans, get others involved in reading the map rather than just following your directions.

Too many leaders use different maps than their employees use when they create strategies and provide directions for execution. More accurate interpretations occur when leaders check their maps with others – a process Senge calls "creating common mental models."[36]

Engage others in discussions about what they see from their position in the organization. How does the landscape look to them? What are the biggest mountains to climb? Where are the easy paths forward?

---

[36] Senge, P. M. (1990). *The Fifth Discipline: The Art & Practice of the Learning Organization.* New York: Doubleday/Currency.

Good navigation helps with execution. Very few organizational landscapes are perfectly flat, and business is more like a cross-country run than a racetrack. As part of your navigational role, you can help your teams prepare for the hills and take advantage of the downhill runs.

One of the biggest challenges for companies is to stay on track. The sport of orienteering, sometimes called cunning running, has developed an extensive collection of tools and a language for navigating across all kinds of landscapes. Most of it was developed before the invention of GPS. Here are a few examples:

Accurate bearings. Success can cause companies to head off in strange directions. Previously, we have looked at the value of a clear vision of where we are going, but it pays to be precise with your bearings (direction on the compass).

I once wasted a lot of a group's time when, overconfident, I didn't check my bearing as I descended from a peak. We went down the wrong ridgeline and had to backtrack. Embarrassing.

Make sure that you are clear on the direction and that the others concur before you set off.

Drift. People tend to take the easiest path, which may not be where you want to go. When traversing slopes, there is a tendency to drift downhill because it's easier. Re-climbing a hill later, however, saps energy and morale.

Promote a discipline around quality to avoid rework.

Handrails. These are landform features, such as trails, rivers, and fence-lines, that you can easily follow, which will send you in the right general direction. They also serve as boundaries. Spending authority limits, policies, regulations, and corporate values are examples of organizational handrails.

Establish handrails with team members to get them moving in the right direction while allowing them some freedom. Create flexibility in a framework.

The path of least resistance. The shortest distance between two points may be a straight line, but it doesn't mean it's the quickest. Traveling cross-country and blazing a path may burn a lot of energy. It is no good being first to market if you can't recoup the investment costs with higher prices or by being first to volume.

An important role of leadership is helping the organization avoid dangerous paths. Overcommitment can be very dangerous in the outdoors, but it has also destroyed businesses. Some of the things that get organizations onto the wrong path are misreading the landscape, personal ego, being overconfident, underestimating challenges, and being unwilling to accept failure. "Sunk cost" is the tendency to irrationally keep investing energy, time, or resources because of a past psychological or physical commitment, regardless of whether it makes sense to keep doing so. It is both a major cause of safety issues in the outdoors and of poor decisions in the corporate world.

I experienced some of these factors when two other cavers and I rafted the underground storm water system beneath Hobart, a small town in Tasmania, Australia, during a creek flood. Hobart is known for its wet climate.

At the time our story begins, it had been raining almost nonstop for over a week. I was attending a caving club meeting with a group of testosterone-fuelled guys. Boredom can lead to inappropriate risk-taking, both in the outdoors and in the executive boardroom. So when someone happened to mention that Hobart had an extensive underground storm water (not sewer) system, the next logical question was:

"Can we explore it?"

"Yes."

"Can we raft it?!"

(cont'd)

That is how I found myself standing beside a swollen creek in a suburban backyard, holding a small inflatable mattress that I had used on previous river trips. The others used a small inflatable raft.

The first two minutes were fun. We spun dizzily past people's backyards on flooded brown creek waters. (No, this was not a safe practice.) Then we entered the storm-water pipes, cutting off our retreat route. We could not paddle upstream against the fast water. It was pitch black, smooth-sided, and completely enclosed. The only way out was through. To say that we had underestimated the challenges and that we were inappropriately confident would have been a massive understatement.

Still, the experience was exhilarating. I was in the lead on my air mattress, hurtling through the darkness. I tried to scrape my hands on the sides to slow down but to no avail. To make matters worse, we had been warned that a grate extended across the lower half of the pipes, close to the exit. In the pitch-blackness, I wondered how a grasshopper felt as it hit the grill of a speeding car.

An occasional, surreal beam of light stabbed into the darkness as we passed an overhead grate exposed to the surface, but the connection to the outside world was gone again within seconds. Forever time finally ended when the pipe opened up into a concrete trough. We managed to scramble out onto the footpath to the astonished looks of suit-wearing businesspeople hiding underneath their umbrellas. Somehow we had missed the grate, and luck had won out over our lack of common sense. We had overcommitted; we had burned our bridges, but we had been very lucky.

How do you avoid overcommitment?

Decide if it makes sense to enter a no-retreat situation. Be very wary of do-or-die situations. As in the outdoors, there are usually chances to come back later when the weather clears or the river drops.

1. *Decide up front what you are willing to pay.*

2. *Know your escape routes. In our case, our only way out was through the pipes.*

3. *Determine if a chain of events is building against you, and determine a cutoff point. Build gates into the project design to force a periodic reevaluation of risks and rewards.*

4. *Do whatever you can to reduce ego as a safety factor. Reframe courage as the capacity to either kill projects or advance them.*

5. *Avoid moving forward just because of sunk cost. Evaluate the project from where it stands and what else it requires rather than what it has cost to date.*

The leader as captain. For particularly chaotic environments, an appropriate leadership analogy might be the captain of a raft crew. The captain is responsible for the direction, steering, choosing who sits where, aligning the crew, what equipment to take, what challenges to take on, and what to avoid. While captains may use a directive style in the midst of the worst whitewater chaos, they will use other leadership styles at other times.

As a rafting instructor, I used all four of Hersey and Blanchard's leadership styles – directing, coaching, supporting, and delegating[37] – to build skills of novice rafters to the point where they could safely guide their own raft through Class-III rapids. I would give directives until the crew gained some understanding of how their paddles, the boat, and the water interacted. The directives were delivered in a clear, crisp style with simple language. "Stop!" "Paddle harder!" A discussion was not invited. Compliance was expected. I then used debriefing to provide coaching and feedback to build their skills further. "Do remember when you...?" "What was your intent?" "What actually happened?" "What could you do differently next time?"

---

[37] Hersey, P. & Blanchard, K. H. (1977). *Management of Organizational Behavior: Utilizing Human Resources.* (3rd ed.) Englewood Cliffs, NJ: Prentice Hall.

In urgent situations when the task is simple, everyone has the same goal, results are what matters most, and there is no need for a debate, then using the directing style saves time, eliminates confusion, and gets the job done. Overuse, however, can leave people feeling disempowered, and it can deprive people of the opportunity to develop, eventually limiting the capabilities of both the individual and group.

Using debriefing to provide coaching and feedback takes longer, but it builds skill in the person who is coached and sends a message that the leader values that person's development. Simple tasks, or parts of tasks, can then be delegated, freeing up the leader's time for higher-level or more strategic tasks.

Using a supporting style, I would sit beside captains-in-training as they took command. My role here was to support their confidence and respond to their requests for support, but not to take back their role.

Use the supporting style when employees have the skills but waver in their confidence, especially as new challenges occur. In this style, you are communicating that your door is open if they need help, but you are less hands-on and not checking in as frequently.

Finally, I would step out of the boat and delegate the command to the captains while following behind in a safety boat. Using this style, I would remain responsible for their performance, but the biggest part of my challenge was to stay out of their way to avoid eroding their confidence or authority with their crew.

Delegation does not mean you abdicate responsibility for how those people perform. The people you appoint as captains over projects should know the performance expectations, values, processes, procedures, level of authority, timing, resources, and spending limits that shape the boundaries of how they get the job done. Ideally, however, the methods, management of subtasks, and leadership of their people should be theirs to determine.

The leader as architect. Organizational language like structure, design, and span of control shapes this metaphor. Organizational charts are the equivalents of architectural blueprints. As architects and designers, leaders try to create a home for the various organizational families with fixed walls, a set number of rooms, and set functions for each of the rooms. This rigidity means that sometimes some rooms are left empty while other rooms are overcrowded. Some parts receive expensive renovations; others are neglected.

Whole industries have grown up around organizational design and reengineering. But organizations don't operate along the neatly drawn lines of their organizational charts. It might help to think more flexibly about the work structures we create. Project teams, for example, are temporary structures. We want to get them up and running quickly, but they are not intended as permanent structures.

In the outdoors, there is a wide variety of shelters and structures that serve many different purposes. In the forest, an overnight shelter can be a bunch of branches and leaves placed up against a tree trunk. In snowstorms, I have slept with ease the whole night just in a bivouac bag or in snow trenches, snow caves, and snow holes, which take just a little more time to build. Vern Tejas, the first person to complete a solo winter ascent of Denali (20,322 feet) and return alive, used a combination of these methods.

Every kind of structure has its strengths and limitations. Tents are quick to pitch, for example, but foundations are important. Tents are not designed as balloons, but I once watched someone's mountain shelter go sailing across a valley in high winds because it had not been anchored correctly.

When did you last check that your organizational design is fit for its purpose?

Avoid restructuring too often, though. Many leaders opt to restructure when they should be working on the culture. For example, if there is with low organic growth in mergers and acquisitions, it may indicate that it's a culture that has lost the energy or desire to innovate and that they are trying to stimulate earnings through M&A cost savings. Restructuring efforts may realize short-term cost savings, but the disruption of moving house too often leads to negative long-term impacts on employee morale, organizational effectiveness, and financial performance.

> Sometimes structures that appear to be solid can provide a false sense of security. While mountain biking down the Yukon, I passed a cabin that had been ripped apart by grizzlies in search of food – fortunately while the owner was elsewhere. The bears had ripped the logs apart at the joints. The owner had not known to embed solid six-inch nails across the joints. More tragically, Three Johns Hut in New Zealand's Southern Alps was reportedly named after three Aussies named John, who were killed when strong winds lifted the hut off its foundations and blew it into the glacier below.

Make sure your organizational structure has a solid cultural foundation and that it's integrated and supported. What values, structure, and culture is your foundation made up of? Is your structure flexible enough for changing conditions?

The leader-sponsor metaphor. The challenge today is not so much to climb Everest or explore the depths of the sea, but rather to find a way to pay for it all. There's an avalanche of proposals flooding into Fortune 500 marketing departments. Pity the poor brand manager who tries to pitch a Mount Everest expedition to management.[38]

Leaders face similar challenges, especially in the middle of the daily noise of organizational life and competing priorities.

How do you get people to sponsor your ideas and plans with their energy and support? One way is to *link your efforts to others' personal needs to have meaningful work, a sense of life purpose, and positive relationships with others.* All of these are elements of spiritual well-being.

---

[38] Blumenfeld, J. (2014). *Get Sponsored: A Funding Guide for Explorers, Adventurers, and Would-Be World Travelers.* New York, NY: Skyhorse Publishing.

In my Ph.D. research, I found a strong connection between spiritual well-being, employee engagement, and business outcomes such as return to shareholders, profitability, and growth. (I am using spirituality in a very broad sense here, not referring to any particular religion or absence of belief in a higher power).

Linking your requests for sponsorship and support to others' needs is one of the keys to moving people from a state of *have to*, to *ought to* (there is a reasonable transaction between us), to *want to*. This shift from engaging people's hands to engaging their heads and eventually their hearts is one way to align individual, team, and organizational needs.

One of the simplest tools for increasing engagement is the concept of the emotional bank account popularized by Stephen Covey in *The 7 Habits of Highly Effective People: Restoring the Character Ethic*. Just as we have a financial bank account, we also have an emotional bank account with others. Each of our interactions makes a deposit or withdrawal from our account with that person.[39]

A synthesis of research by John Gottman and Nan Silver in *Why Marriages Succeed or Fail: What You Can Learn From the Breakthrough Research to Make Your Marriage Last*, Aubrey Daniels in *Bringing Out the Best in People: How to Apply the Astonishing Power of Positive Reinforcement*, and others suggest that when the ratio of deposits to withdrawals drops below about 3:1, a relationship will start to decline. When the ratio gets above about 5:1, that relationship starts to thrive. If the relationship is at an early stage, and the first contact is a big withdrawal, it can take 26 positive deposits to repair the relationship. Consequently, if your first contact with a new supplier, manager, employee, or another stakeholder is a significant withdrawal, you will have to do a lot of work to repair the relationship.

---

[39] Covey, S.R. (2004) *The 7 Habits of Highly Effective People: Restoring the Character Ethic*. ([Rev. ed.].). New York, NY: Fireside Books.

The concept of the emotional bank account is very useful for promoting positive reinforcement. But it does require that you invest time in learning what constitutes a deposit or withdrawal for another person. Check out Gary Chapman and Paul White's book *The 5 Languages of Appreciation in the Workplace: Empowering Organizations by Encouraging People* or Bob Nelson's *1501 Ways to Reward People* for ideas on how to maximize the power of non-monetary awards.

A colleague of mine is a managing director for a consulting group. She prefers to receive praise in private, but the group she inherited when she acceded the position was accustomed to receiving praise in public. Following her preferences, she would bring people into her office for private praise – something I imagine may also have created some fear at first! After a while, her team commented that they appreciated the private praise but asked why she never recognized them in public. She had simply been applying her preferences to the group. By doing so, she had been undermining the value of her deposits.

Research by Gallup points to five common desires employees have that managers can impact: trust, hope that things will improve over time, a sense of stability, order and justice, and compassion (does my manager understand and empathize with my situation and challenges?). Here are some principles that support effective use of the emotional bank account concept:

1. *Make deposits before you need to make withdrawals*

2. *Know what constitutes a deposit or withdrawal for the employees*

3. *Deposit rewards in a currency that has value for them*

4. *Ensure your rewards are commensurate with the risks and efforts that your employees expend.*

Employees, managers, customers, and suppliers are all potential sponsors. What will you do this week to make a deposit into a sponsor's account? What questions can you ask someone this week to learn what constitutes a deposit or withdrawal for them?

What metaphor do you use for your role as a leader? Is it the most powerful metaphor for getting you where you want to go and being the leader you want to be? If not, what experiences might you set up to test out a new role? How will that role shape your agenda, values, and activities? What should you focus on in order to support that role? What are others' (managers, peers, reports, stakeholders) expectations of your role?

Small steps

1. *Clarify what types of leadership roles will both leverage your strengths and meet the expectations of your organization. Allow space for team members to take on other leadership roles.*

2. *Be clear on the decision-making style you are using. For example, don't seek input if you have already made your decision.*

3. *Build positive relationships with external stakeholders to help your team stay connected to the bigger picture and protect them when necessary.*

4. *If you manage a virtual team, remember to create common spaces, artifacts, and connections to replace face-to-face opportunities and strengthen the team identity.*

5. *If you are taking on a new team, facilitate early opportunities for the team members to ask questions and get to know you and vice versa. Questions might address, for example, vision, priorities, personal interests, leadership style, or expectations.*

CHAPTER 7

Execution

Warren Bennis, widely regarded as one of the pioneers of contemporary leadership studies, defined leadership as "the capacity to translate vision into reality." Execution is not simply getting a lot done. It is getting the right things done, efficiently, and at the right time. Execution-focused leadership is also about creating momentum and staying on track.

Organizations with great execution create a discipline and cadence around the execution by continuously revisiting their focus and prioritizing their goals and actions according to their vision. The members of the organizations understand the wider business context and know how their contributions support the organizations' success. Roles and responsibilities are well defined. They set stretch targets on a regular basis, and there is a culture of learning and improvement.

Organizations with great execution move differently than those without it, just as a competent rock climber moves differently than a beginner. Sailors, rafters, kayakers, skiers, and mountain bikers need great skill in timing to execute well. So do great businesses. Let us look at some aspects of execution in more detail.

Cadence

One of my first work experiences was working on an assembly line where the highest priority, apparently, was to look busy. When a delay further up the line caused me to run out of work, my supervisor directed me to start undoing the work I had recently done. I resigned the next day.

Often in business, it is "wait, wait, wait, GO!" A steady pace is usually better than a rush and rest approach, but there are times when rapid speed pays big dividends, just like in the outdoors.

In the mountains, moving too quickly can cause sweating, which is particularly dangerous in cold environments. Rushing also increases the likelihood of mistakes, and it consumes more energy. Mountaineers use the concept of the "rest step" to provide microbreaks while maintaining momentum. By using rest steps, they avoid rushing and the need for long recoveries.

Increase your productivity at work by taking frequent microbreaks of 30 seconds at your desk to stretch and refocus.

Set up a regular cadence, or milestone tripwires, for project reviews, training, and other core business processes. This can be more challenging for groups that are highly dependent on the demands or requests of others. Increase control of your workflow by investing the time to build a trusted-advisor relationship where you have a seat at the table, rather than just being a pair of hands.

Effectiveness

Execution is also about effectiveness. Cross-ocean rowers like Roz Savage and polar explorers like Fridtjof Nansen frequently described days or weeks when they rowed or sailed hard but made little or no progress towards their goals because of currents or wind. Similarly, there is a big difference between progress and nonproductive change. The latter is too common in organizations. Frequently it is fueled by new leaders who want to make their marks, regardless of whether or not it builds effectively on the work of their predecessors.

Ensure that your metrics measure progress in the right direction, not just activity.

Timing

In the book of Ecclesiastes, it says: "For everything there is a season, a time for every activity under heaven" (Ecclesiastes 3:1, New Living Translation). Timing is a key aspect of effective execution. Knowing what season you are in and the rhythms of different landscapes, whether natural or human, can help you use your time and energy effectively. You don't want to be a victim of bad timing – like the big bush turkey that wandered along the scrub of a creek line and showed up on my doorstep one Thanksgiving morning.

Spend any time in the outdoors, and you will quickly appreciate the difference between time and timing. How and when you get things done depend on the season or the rhythms of the sun, moon, and tides. The Yukon River in Alaska, for example, is an ice highway during winter, so it connects remote towns via snowmobiles. But in the summer, you need a boat or plane to get to the same towns. In Borneo in the early morning, I safely crossed jungle rivers that became dangerous torrents once afternoon thunderstorms hit. You will save a lot of sweat if you hike the desert in the cooler periods of the day.

What is not possible today may be possible tomorrow as the season changes or the environment evolves. New technology, emerging markets, and shifts in demography are occurring all the time. Improvements in navigational aids, communications, and equipment have fueled dramatic advances in almost every outdoor sport. A successful launch of a new product may depend as much on timing and how you address external conditions as on internal organizational willpower.

The Greeks differentiated between chronos (chronological) time and kairos time (the right or opportune moment). Whether we chase billable hours or quality time with our kids, there never seems to be enough time. And yet we respond almost instantly to the addictive chimes of the latest text message or email.

Would you be more effective if you invested a little more attention on kairos time instead of chronos time?

With relationships, we miss the idea of timing our messages because we are more sensitized to chronos time than peoples' readiness. Change management projects are frequently declared complete based on a calendar date but often with people left disengaged or resistant. Following are some examples of timing that make sense across outdoor, personal and organizational landscapes.

There is a time to start. Too many people miss opportunities because they never get started. The challenge of overcoming perceived or actual risks can cause hesitation. Mark Zuckerberg, one of the founders of Facebook, said: "The biggest risk is not taking any risk. In a world that's changing really quickly, the only strategy that is guaranteed to fail is not taking risks."

Overcoming inertia is essential to leadership success whatever the situation. Henry David Thoreau, after living in the woods for over two years, observed:

> I learned this, at least, by my experiment; that if one advances confidently in the direction of his dreams, and endeavors to live the life which he has imagined, he will meet with a success unexpected in common hours.[40]

Movement and action are antidotes to inertia and inaction if done wisely. On Denali (20,320 feet), our climbing team was plagued by poor weather and snow conditions that made making a bid for the summit a gamble. Eventually, we decided to set out on a reconnaissance climb. Although it did not lead immediately to a summit experience, we used the information we gained to help us get to the top a few days later. It also served as an opportunity to train the group in team movement and polish our safety processes.

Use safe, small experiments or reconnaissance expeditions to help you gain momentum, information, and skills for a more comprehensive expedition or project.

It's also possible to set out confidently and have the ground collapse below you. Snow bridges can look quite solid, yet when you cross them, you can

---

[40]   Thoreau, H.D. (1854). *Walden; or, Life in the Woods.* Boston, MA: Ticknor and Fields.

suddenly find yourself spinning in space wrapped between walls of cold blue ice. Cross snow bridges when temperatures are colder and the snow is firmer.

Mountaineers frequently travel on tricky terrain. It's often necessary if you want to get anywhere. Business leaders also need to know how to manage risks. The outdoors is a great arena for learning how to take smart risks and building judgment. You can still, for example, navigate political crevasses (a frequent barrier to execution) by applying the following principles:

1. *Read the terrain.* Don't go in the blind. Working your way through a crevasse field in a whiteout is dangerous. You may be better off digging in and waiting for the winds to shift and the visibility to clear.

2. *Ask about recent conditions.* Talk with local experts or other people who have been there recently. Know what the political weather forecast is.

3. *Travel with others.* Build alliances and supporters. Have a champion or mentor who can help you look out for places that are unstable or help catch you if you fall.

4. *Practice a variety of strategies for negotiating tough terrain.* You can jump over small crevasses. Larger ones you may have to go around.

There is a time to say no. It is one of the most valuable and most difficult skills for a leader to learn. But it is vital in order to maintain focus on the essential activities and help people use their time, energy, and motivation wisely. One of the most common complaints employees have is that there are too many priorities and that those priorities keep shifting.

Align rewards with the quality of the results, not the number of activities.

Sometimes, saying no can also save lives. I was scheduled to lead a mountaineering course in Washington State. We had time restrictions, we had traveled at least 300 miles, and we were eager to head up the mountain. Overnight, though, we had some snowfall. We tried to assess the risk of an avalanche, but it was a borderline decision. In the end, I called off the climb.

As we were packing up to leave, we heard a large rumble and saw a rising white cloud of an avalanche. It had swept right across our intended route.

It can be hard to say no if you dash people's dreams by doing so. It helps to remember that saying no often means saying yes to something else – in this case, the team's safety.

There is a time to retreat. One of the first mountains I attempted to climb was Mount Cook, New Zealand's highest peak at 12,218 feet. I had planned to hike solo across a snowy pass to the West Coast when I ran into an Australian Special Forces commando looking for a climbing partner. I did not have the proper equipment – no helmet or headlamp and tramping boots rather than mountaineering boots – but I thought I could improvise.

Two Kiwis and six Japanese climbers, whom we had shared some good Japanese whiskey with down in the valley, beat us out the door of the staging hut at 1:30 a.m.

Things went well initially, as the snow was hard and moonlight lit up the glacier. We made good time (the Linda Glacier Route on Cook, rated moderate, takes an average of 15 to 18 hours to complete and is subject to a variety of hazards including crevasses, ice- and rockfall, avalanche, and adverse weather). The final approach to the summit involved climbing an ice gully. Because of the risk of ice- and rockfall from those climbing above us, we chose to wait in a crevasse while the others made their final push.

While huddling to keep warm, we became alarmed by a significant storm coming in from the coast (weather forecasting was much less reliable at that time). There was nothing to stop the wind on its journey all the way from South Africa until it hit the Southern Alps, where rapid updrafts would then wreak havoc on the slopes with extreme winds and heavy precipitation.

(cont'd)

Nevertheless, we were not far from the top. I struggled deeply with the decision. I was very motivated since it would be my first significant mountain, but in the end, we could not justify the risk. We could see the clouds boiling up, and we knew we should retreat quickly. On the descent, we became enveloped in a whiteout. We could barely make out our tracks at our feet.

By the time we reached the relative flatness of the glacier, the wind was in full force. It repeatedly knocked us off our feet, and we had to belay each other even on flat ground, leaning on the rope to make progress. We staggered into the hut, extremely grateful for the refuge. The wind continued to increase, picking up small rocks and pelting them against the hut walls.

Slightly rejuvenated, we took a couple of forays out of the hut to see if we could locate the others, but it was impossible in the whiteout and shrieking wind. The two Kiwis stumbled into the hut a few hours later, but the Japanese were forced to overnight in the storm. Of the six of them, only three survived. Two were apparently blown off the mountain after they failed to "anchor" once their rappels were finished. A third climber died of hypothermia.

I helped one of the survivors fill out the accident report. The sunk cost played a big part in this accident as it has in many others. The group had been close to the end of their available vacation time and did not know when they would be able to return. The time and distance to travel added to their ill-fated decision to push on. We lived to climb another day and recycled our experiences on other climbs.

I recently helped design and facilitate a global kickoff meeting for the restart of a multi-billion-dollar JV Capital project that had been put on hold. It seems to be an exception that projects are appropriately put on hold, but the leaders had gained tremendous respect and credibility from the team for postponing the launch until the right time. Too many projects are advanced because of sunk cost when they should be shut down. Leaders' egos and sense of infallibility are often contributing factors.

Lessons from my Mount Cook climb:

- *Watch for signs of overinvestment in goals by yourself and others – overly optimistic projections, over-allocation of time or energy compared to a project's priority, or ongoing appeals for more money, more time, and more resources.*
- *Create a culture where people are rewarded for saying no, not just yes. Include a "black hat" (pessimistic thinking) role into your decision-making processes at the right time.*
- *Use outsiders' perspectives to help you avoid sunk cost issues.*
- *Find ways to recycle time and resource investments to reduce pressure to push on inappropriately. The time and energy I invested in my Mount Cook climb were learning for future, harder climbs. Design work on an engineering project might become a template for a future capital project.*
- *To avoid projects going off the rails, determine in advance where you will break a negative chain of events.*
- *Review timelines and other constraints to ensure they are not arbitrary. Not all projects are as urgent as others.*

There is a time to play safe. One of the biggest risks of climbing in New Zealand is being caught in an avalanche. The risk usually increases later in the day as the sun heats up the slopes. So when three others and I set out to climb Aiguille Rouge, we started well before light as most climbers do. I remember Aiguille Rouge as a soaring line up a narrow rock ridge. It overlooks the Malte Brun Range with Mount Cook, New Zealand's highest peak, hovering in the distance.

After the sun had risen, we observed signs that indicated a high risk of an avalanche that day. The sun gave off a lot of heat even early in the day. We saw small snow sloughs from the previous days, and when we threw snowballs, they rolled for a distance before stopping. We all noted the danger and predicted that the snow slopes would get dicey later that day. We would need to stay off them and pick a longer, safer route down a rock ridge.

(cont'd)

The exposure off the ridge was sobering, and the rock was slightly loose, but we made it safely to the top after a long climb, and we stopped to drink in the view. At that point, the other pair decided that they wanted to get back to the hut quickly and see if they could get a plane out a day earlier. Despite our previous conversations about the risk of avalanche, they decided to take the faster and seemingly easier route down the big snow slope. We were unable to change their minds, but my climbing partner and I chose to follow the rock ridge down until we were safely out of the danger zone of possible avalanches.

If your original goals are inappropriate, it is easy to create a "slippery slope" situation where you inappropriately revise your original standards. In our case, there was no pressing need to get down quickly, and the biggest goal of the other pair of climbers should have been getting down safely.

From our vantage point on the nearby ridge, my partner and I watched as the others triggered an avalanche right at their feet. They lucked out, though, and were able to jump to the side just before things got rolling. Initially, we thought that the avalanche was rather small. Later we could see that we had badly underestimated its scale. The slide had gone downhill at least 900 feet, and what we thought were small boulders were 20 to 40 feet cliffs buried in debris.

The others eventually made it to the base of the climb after traversing over to the route we had taken. They had put themselves in danger, but they also wound up expending far more time and energy than we did.

Doing things right the first time usually saves time and energy, both in the mountains and in business.

To avoid the "slippery slope" phenomenon, take the time to look back at your original intent periodically and see how far you have drifted off course.

One company that learned this lesson of maintaining operational discipline is BP. The costs of not maintaining a safety culture nearly drove them to bankruptcy after the oil spill in the Gulf of Mexico. The whole company is now under dramatically increased pressure to operate safely, but they still have the pressures of managing costs and restarting production globally in order to deliver on promises made to shareholders.

Do you pay the price up front to invest in extra safety, or will you be paying for the potential loss of life, damage to the brand, and drop in stock price afterward? In the mountains, are you willing to put the energy into taking a longer route to avoid known hazards?

There is a time to be open to the path less traveled. Robert Frost wrote:

Two roads diverged in a wood, and I –
I took the one less traveled by,
And that has made all the difference.[41]

I had just been hired by a company to create and deliver leadership development programs when, unfortunately, a global oversupply of product built up, and the company started multiple rounds of layoffs. Those layoffs, which caught me in the final round, cut 55% of the workforce and slashed our department from 342 to 43.

I received a minimal termination package. Years of working with nonprofits and paying my way through grad school had left me with very limited savings. I had just managed to get my Green Card three weeks before being laid off. Otherwise, I would have had 10 days to find another similar job, or I would be forced to leave the country. This all happened at the height of the recession.

Despite my situation, I decided to start my own business and create my own security rather than chasing another corporate job. Given my financial position at the time, it's perhaps surprising that I took the riskiest and less traveled path, but I had my backpack, and it made all the difference.

(cont'd)

---

41   Frost, R. (1921). *Mountain Interval*. New York, NY: H. Holt and Co.

My backpack, in this context, is my personal metaphor for resourcefulness. There is a difference between resources and resourcefulness. In my 20s, I had left New Zealand with just a backpack, a few hundred dollars, and a promise of a low-paying temporary job. You can carry a limited amount in a backpack, but resourcefulness weighs nothing.

Although I had limited resources, my spirit at the time of the layoffs was ready to set out on the road less traveled, regardless of rational calculus. I put my trust in my resourcefulness rather than my resources. It has made all the difference. I now have more money, fun, freedom, and travel experiences, and I have met and worked with great people along the way. I feel very fortunate.

If nothing else, adventurous experiences can provide you with metaphorical life anchors that provide a sense of stability.

What life-anchor experiences can provide stability for you? Use your life history to help you be resourceful when you lack resources.

There is a time to reap. If you have taken the time to sow by investing in building customer relationships, training staff, and equipment, there will also come a time to reap. Sometimes you reap from your efforts, other times you reap just because life presents opportunities. Those opportunities sometimes come disguised as pigs, which can look unattractive.

Our Army reconnaissance squad was on a survival training exercise. Of course, we had no rations, and the exfiltration point was dozens of miles away when we came across a wild boar and a litter of piglets. We were tired and hungry from our lack of food. Somehow we managed to separate three piglets from their mother. They were surrounded and summarily dispatched with drawn bayonets and roasted over a camouflage-concealed fire. Bush tucker always tastes good. The piglets supplied us with the extra calories we needed to pick up the pace and get to the finish line early.

123

Sometimes we wrestle with whether or not to take advantage of opportunities that present themselves. Some opportunities are potential distractions. George Bernard Shaw wrote: "I learned long ago, never to wrestle with a pig. You get dirty, and besides, the pig likes it." Unlike Shaw, I think that a part of execution leadership is wrestling with pigs and deciding whether they are too slippery or whether they will feed your team.

What are the pigs you are wrestling with now? Pigs are unattractive; bacon is delicious. *Learn to distinguish between opportunities and traps.*

Look for creative ways to turn traps into opportunities.

Oysters provide good energy, but chipping them off the rocks burns more calories than they provide. Australia's Aborigines solved that problem by laying grass over the top of oyster beds at low tide and setting fire to the grass. The oysters popped open with the heat and were ready to eat with minimal effort.

A mate and I hooked two black marlins one afternoon while fishing in a small runabout off the Sydney coastline. My mate, now a pro fisherman, estimated one at 250 pounds and the other at 350 pounds. It was like watching the movie The Old Man and the Sea. The fish alternately charged underneath the boat, ripped out the line while diving deep, and exploded through the surface while shaking their heads trying to loosen the hook. Despite our best efforts, we were not able to land either fish. We had hooked them on 30-pound handlines while jigging with lures for bottom fish.

Make sure you are equipped to take advantage of opportunities that come your way.

There is a time to commit. Cherry Tree Creek is California's toughest commercially-rafted Class-V river. It is a superb trip for kayakers. The water is cold and clear but hides a range of challenges including angled hydraulics that test kayakers' attention, and places where the current flows under big boulders ready to punish boaters who don't follow the right line or have a strong Eskimo roll. Many rapids are very technical, so precise boat control is required to avoid flips or sudden drops. Paddling Cherry Tree Creek is a masterclass in the nature of commitment. Here are a few lessons:

Decisiveness is mandatory in big-water situations. There are places to pause and scan the river ahead, but once you make a decision, you must commit. After launching, the creek enters a steep canyon, so the only way out is through. Know what you are committing to and that you have the skills and resources you need. Companies without a decisive plan of action will get pushed around by business currents and potentially capsized, trapped, or wrecked.

Once on the water, you must take control. On easier rivers, and in some marketplaces, you can just drift along with the current. Not so on Cherry Tree Creek. In whitewater, you gain control by moving either faster or slower than the current. Both approaches have tradeoffs. Going at the same speed lets the river take control and is a form of non-commitment.

Back-paddling to slow the boat and buy time can consume a lot of energy. This is an all-day trip, so you can't paddle flat out the whole time. Similarly, your people will lose commitment if you expect them to paddle flat out all the time. The challenge of going faster is that it reduces the time you have to make decisions about upcoming threats. Go too fast in business and you may be ahead of the market. The trick is to know when to hold back and when to commit. That comes down to a kayaker's ability to read the water and a leader's knowledge of their industry and its rhythms.

At work, do you tend to go faster or slower than the current? What does your organizational and strategic situation warrant? What can you do to build flexibility in your pacing? A few examples would be:

- *Apply Pareto's 80/20 rule to information gathering. According to this rule, 80% of your misdirected efforts will only get you 20% of the results. Conversely, 20% of the right information will get you 80% of the results. What is enough information to make a reasonable judgment?*

- *Check whether you are setting arbitrarily fast completion dates. Do you sacrifice quality when there is no real urgency?*
- *Can you work on project items in parallel rather than in series to reduce the overall timeline?*

Being overcommitted can be a safety risk in the outdoors. It is usually connected to a lack of flexibility, preparedness, skills, or resources. However, being too tentative in whitewater can be just as dangerous as being reckless. Paddle too slowly into a stopper, and you can get swamped. It can also be demotivating, since you are losing energy fighting the current. Competitors may swamp businesses that are too slow to market. Business strategists employ both faster and slower approaches in different markets. The former equates to innovation leadership or time to volume; the latter equates to a strategy of learning from market leaders and copying efficiently.

Commitment, or lack of it, by kayakers can be observed in their paddle strokes. Shallow or tentative moves often indicate that the kayakers are uncertain or feel off balance. When leaders are driving change, how deeply they put their paddles into the water and how broadly they reach may be an indicator of how committed they are and can determine the success of the effort. Change management efforts sometimes fail when employees interpret leaders' tentative actions as a lack of commitment or conviction. Employees decide to ride out the next rapid rather than paddle through the waves.

What are your actions telling your people about your level of commitment?

You can set and sell the direction, or you can engage others in creating the plan. Just make sure that everyone knows where you are going when you push off and that everyone is paddling together.

One of the more powerful kayaking strokes is the sweep stroke. It involves the paddler leaning far out and scribing a semi-circle on the water. It turns a kayak quickly, but in initiating the turn, it looks as though the boat may capsize, just as many change efforts look unstable in the early stages.

126

The stability of the stroke lies in the committing reach of the paddlers, their capacity to lean into the water (which holds the blade up), the weight of the paddlers on the blade, and a strong follow-through. Other even more powerful and quicker strokes get their power from going deep into the water, the equivalent to challenging deep undercurrents of a corporate culture.

What does not work, except in the easiest waters, are tentative, non-committal actions that have neither reach nor depth. Commitment to the goal and flexibility in approach are powerful counterintuitive partners, but they increase your ability to navigate life's whitewater successfully. Kayakers need to be committed to the correct line on the river to avoid hazards and must use a wide variety of paddle strokes and maneuvers to get there.

As a leader, you need to be clear on the line you are taking but be ready to adjust your tactics in how you get there. How far out are you willing to reach to change direction? It impacts how quickly you can turn the boat. Try a different demographic or geographic market for your product. If you can't seem to sell an idea, find a sponsor, or if people seem unwilling to make a big change, break the change down into small pieces. A raft can be re-directed by lots of small paddle strokes, or by a few powerful ones.

There is a right time to celebrate – but don't celebrate prematurely. The summit is not the end of the climb. The time to celebrate is when you have returned safely to base camp, when the contract is signed, or when the check is cashed. A premature celebration can risk progress in organizational change efforts, but it can be deadly in the mountains. In mountaineering, it comes in the form of people switching off, getting careless, and discounting the increased risks on the way down.

There is a natural tendency to celebrate when you have reached the top of the mountain, when you have signed the merger deal, or when you have installed the new software. But if the software is not used, or the merger does not reap the intended results, were you successful? If you get to the top of a mountain but die on the way down, is that success? If you complete a project on time but burn out your team and half of them leave, is that success?

More climbers die on the way down than up. More projects fail in the sustaining phase than the initiating phase. With the emphasis on metrics and accountability in many corporations today, there is an increasing tendency to want to tick the boxes, declare victory, and get on to the next project that has been waiting for attention. What suffers is the sustaining phase of the new change or project. Why do so many employees now feel that they can simply wait out the latest fad? Leaders may be modeling that they are more concerned about checking the box rather than ensuring that the change sticks.

Are your metrics, feedback, and compensation rewarding change that sticks or merely boxes checked?

There is a time to follow through. One part of returning home is cleaning up. Gear has to be cleaned, repaired, and inventoried for use in the next expedition. It may not be you who uses it next, so it is especially important that you don't leave a mess for others to find and clean up.

As a young trainee officer, when I returned from the field, I allowed myself to get distracted halfway through cleaning up my mess kit. My drill sergeant and commanding officer found plenty to comment on, with very explicit language, a week later when it was time for our weekly inspection. A colorful science experiment stared back at them as they dove into my pack and found my petri dish of food remains in my mess tin. Five days of confinement to the barracks and several punishment pack drills reinforced the follow-up lesson nicely for me.

Don't leave loose ends on one project as you get drawn into the next one. (A test for how well shift teams respect each other is how well they manage the handoffs and what condition they leave the operating spaces in.)

To support execution and maximize productivity, help teams do the following:

1. Clarify how their work supports the vision and strategy (engagement)

2. Focus on value over activity (effectiveness)

3. Understand or, even better, predict changes in priorities (focus and priorities)

4. Create and maintain a culture of continuous improvement (efficiency)

Small steps

1. *Don't ask people if they understand. Ask them to paraphrase your expectations so that you can check their understanding.*

2. *Use the 80/20 principle to keep focusing on what is important, but remember to balance meeting the needs of other stakeholders. Your 20 could be their 80, and you might need their help in the future.*

3. *Break large tasks down into small chunks to work on so that you can keep the momentum going even when other priorities compete with yours.*

4. *Create a cadence and process for learning (not blaming) from projects to keep improving.*

5. *Ask: "What is the next step we can take to move things forward?"*

CHAPTER 8

Communication

Shane Toohey has extreme skied on seven continents, and he is a co-founder of the innovative consulting group Peak Teams, which specializes in how to inspire, align, engage, and enable employees. He notes: "Communication is the connection between a leader and their followers." It is the central thread between them just as the climbing rope is the thread between a leader and follower.

The biggest driver of employee engagement is an employee's relationship with their manager(s), and communication is obviously central to these relationships. When managers hold the rope too tightly, employees feel micromanaged. When they hold it too loosely, the employees feel no connection and fear that they might take an unprotected fall. Disengagement and turnover are common results of poor relationships between managers and employees. The ability to manage upwards, influence without authority, and work with stakeholders, government agencies, and customers are also greatly impacted. Here are a few communication lessons from the outdoors.

Communicate Your Needs Early

Jim, a colleague, told me the story of how his grandparents nearly got divorced after 30 years of an otherwise apparently happy and successful marriage. It started with the bologna and mayo sandwiches that his grandfather ate while he was dangling hundreds of feet in the air.

It was a classic immigrant's story. Jim's parents came to the U.S. soon after the end of World War II. They only had the clothes on their backs, a few bucks in their pockets, and dreams of a better life. Jim's grandfather was an ironworker who worked without a safety net on narrow steel I-beams hundreds of feet above the ground. He helped lay the steel skeleton that later became one of New York's skyscrapers. **(cont'd)**

They were so poor that all they could afford for his lunch were bologna and mayo sandwiches on plain white bread. His wife lovingly made these sandwiches every day, exactly the same way, for 30 years. So Jim's grandfather went to work each day with his bologna and mayo on white bread sandwiches in his small metal lunch box. He would climb into the air and sling iron beams all morning until the lunch siren sounded. Then he would open his lunch box, and sitting on a four-inch beam hundreds of feet above the ground, he would eat his sandwiches.

After 30 years, one day he said to his wife: "Honey, would you mind putting a little less mayo on my bologna and mayo sandwiches?" Guess what happened? She blew up at him! "What do you mean?" she said. "I've been making those sandwiches exactly the same way year after year. Why are you telling me this just now?" One thing led to another, and, as Jim tells the story, they nearly divorced.

If we think about time as the X-axis and impact as the Y-axis, what would have happened if Jim's grandfather had raised the issue (or his grandmother had checked his preferences) in the first few days? The impact would have been minimal. But since he did not raise the issue for 30 years, the impact was massive.

There are some times when it makes sense to avoid an issue, but more often it risks an escalation.

How many "bologna and mayo sandwich" situations are you failing to address? Not everything is worth speaking up about, but when it is, speak up early before things escalate too far. Some tips for finding managerial courage are:

- *When you notice that an issue keeps getting pushed to the bottom of your to-do list, ask yourself why.*
- *Imagine and feel the increased future impact of postponing addressing the issue.*

- *View challenging issues as opportunities to prepare for handling greater leadership responsibilities. Handling tough issues is an opportunity to build your credibility.*
- *Remember, where there is conflict, there is energy. It tells you what is important to you and the other person, so it is an opportunity to deepen a relationship if handled well.*
- *Focus not just on your own discomfort. If the issue is poor performance, and you are holding back feedback, you are holding back the others' development. That is not fair to them.*

A Tennis Match

People are often very good at communicating from the perspective of their particular discipline. When there is a difference of opinions in approach, timing, or priorities, it sets up what I describe as a tennis match. When group A serves their initial point over the net, they attempt to get their opponent on the back foot. Group B listens to evaluate the other group's argument and find weaknesses, rather than trying to understand or look for points of alignment. Or group B just waits for group A to finish so that they can volley back their pre-prepared remarks. The conversation continues, volley after volley, until one group tires or makes a mistake. If the goal is to win, then we have a result. But what is the result we have achieved? One group has won; they have achieved the best result for their group. But it might not be the best result for the organization overall. The next game has been set up as another oppositional conflict rather than an opportunity to seek alignment and increased understanding of the broader organization. How do we change the game?

When collaboration is the desired outcome, apply the principle, popularized by Stephen Covey, of "seek first to understand and then be understood." Find ways to model alignment rather than opposition.

Getting other people's perspectives first creates a healthier dialogue. Set your intent as understanding their views rather than winning. Open the conversation by inviting them to educate you on their perspectives. Listen to understand rather than evaluate. Ask open-ended questions that funnel down to narrower ones. When they start to run out of steam, ask again if there is anything else you should know. Ask permission to paraphrase what you heard to confirm your understanding is accurate.

Next, ask if you can offer your perspective since you may have different information, experiences, priorities, and so on. When you have finished, don't ask if they understand, since they will almost always think they do. Request that they paraphrase what they heard from you.

Next, merge the two perspectives. Grab a sheet of paper and divide it into three columns: things you agree on, things you need to research more, and things you may need to agree to disagree on. I like to have the sheet of paper in front of both the other person and me and give the pen to the other person. Then the problem is on paper instead of between us.

Starting with points of agreement builds goodwill, alignment, and momentum. Starting with points of disagreement may seem quicker and more efficient, but it more often results in divergence as people create entrenched positions. Sometimes the quickest way to the top of the mountain is not the most direct.

Finally, go for action. Ask the questions a journalist would ask about the plan to move forward: "Who will do what, when, where, why (which addresses motivation), how (if specific policies, principles, or procedures are to be followed), and how well (if certain standards are to be met)?"

Creating the plan together usually leads to greater alignment and commitment to follow through.

Clarity of Intent Versus Impact

Mount Arapiles is a world-class rock-climbing venue in Victoria, Australia. At one point, it had some of the world's hardest climbs. It's the kind of place where climbers connect to push their personal limits.

Climbing is a potentially dangerous sport partly because of communication challenges. (I'll summarize some lessons learned from my experiences at the end of this story.) Rock climbing has developed a standardized vocabulary to help avoid communication issues that can be exacerbated by background wind, calls from other climbers, or the inability to see your partner.

What kinds of background noise are making communication difficult for you?

Pete and I had just met the night before whilst hanging around a communal campfire at Mount Arapiles. We discovered we were both looking for climbing partners. My first climb with Pete was a stretch for me, both in terms of difficulty and it being a significant climb through an overhang. Pete cruised up the wall of a narrow canyon and then shimmied upside down through the overhang like it was nothing, but I knew that even following was not going to be easy for me. I was amazed at how little protection he had placed as he moved through the overhang (that will become important later). I forged up the wall and through the overhang, hanging upside down like a bat. But since I was new to climbing overhangs, I tired quickly.

Suddenly I plummeted 30 feet, then swung in a huge arc and landed – on the other side of the canyon. The climb was now on the opposite side of the canyon. Pete had realized what had happened, and although the fall was a long one, he had held me well.

There was nothing to do but give Pete a heads up and launch myself off the side of the canyon to get back beneath the climb. I now hung in space below the previous piece of protection that Pete had placed. I used prusik cords to climb back up. (The cords are tied with a specialized knot that allows the climber to ascend the main rope but which locks off as a safety device in the event of a climber's fall.) Because I was moving underneath the roof, I had to remove that protection to move forward, but that caused me to take another fall and swing. Three times I prusiked up, pulled out a piece of protection, fell, and swung. (cont'd)

Finally, I struggled up over the lip to see Pete's smart-ass grin. I gave him the digital salute as I collapsed on the ledge. I was glad it was over. Except it wasn't. I thought we would have had an easy walk down the back of the mountain, but Pete informed me that we still had a series of rappels and down-climbing sections. Oh well, down is easy, right?

We rappelled down the first rock wall and met on a ledge. The next section was an easy descent, but what I didn't realize was that there was another section of steep down-climbing below for which we would need the rope. Pete climbed down, out of sight. "It's easy from here," he called up. "Throw the rope."

Have you ever been in one of those situations where you thought you said something very clearly, but the other person interpreted it in a completely different way? Pete was about to have one of those experiences.

I threw the rope – all of it – all the way to the ground far below. I am glad that I couldn't see Pete's face as the rope went sailing by. He had meant, "Throw the rope down to the next ledge." Obviously, we kept it together while free-climbing down the gully, but we didn't have the safety of the rope. It was not all that difficult, but I was very tired, and by the time we got to the bottom, it had started raining, and we were losing light. If it had been a bit later in the day, we could have been in quite a jam.

Here are some lessons from that little escapade:

Remove background noise wherever possible by creating norms around multitasking, cell phones, etc.

For critical communications, check the other person's understanding of your intent, not just your content. Ask: "Can you paraphrase what you heard for me? What was most important to me, why, and how did I feel about it?"

Strive for specificity in conversation by asking the journalist's questions: "Who specifically?" "What specifically?" "When specifically?" "Where specifically?" (the one I missed in the story above), "How specifically?" and "How well?"

Instead of saying that you need to be more of a team, ask more questions such as, "Who is the team you are referring to?" "What are the team behaviors you want to see or hear? and "When do we need to be a team? All the time? In meetings? When representing ourselves externally?"

Corporate communication is full of fuzzy language. Develop a standardized vocabulary among your team members to avoid misunderstandings. Make a list of fuzzy words and clarify their meaning. Explore, for example, whether consensus, teamwork, initiative, and leadership means the same thing for each person.

Pay particular attention to communications at these three key points in relationships: when you are just getting to know someone, when people are in stressful situations, and when you think you know them really well. When onboarding new people, or when you start reporting to a new manager, ask about their communication preferences (or ask their administrative assistant if they have one). Be careful not to shoot the messenger when your team is under stress. To break familiarity, ask employees to share something that others don't know about them, that they are proud of, or tells something important about them.

Expect greater communication challenges when you don't have a line of sight. With fewer visual clues of body language, virtual team members are more at risk of misinterpreting others' messages. Check in more frequently, but explain why you are doing so. Ask more clarifying and confirmatory questions. Compare their answers with other performance indicators like increased absences, late completion of work, or an increase in mistakes.

Speak Their Language

Communication was one of the first critical lessons I learned while dogsledding in a minus-40-degree Fahrenheit classroom. Not communication with the other people, but with the dogs. Apart from the instructors, all of us on the 10-day winter expedition in the Boundary Waters of Minnesota were new to dogsledding. If we couldn't get our dogs to align and collaborate, we would be the ones pulling sleds full of gear through deep snow, which would be very hard work for us.

Well-trained sled dogs, however, love to pull heavy loads. They can do it for hours under horrific weather and snow conditions. They yap excitedly as you hook them into harnesses in the morning. When they take off, they fly across the snow.

I ran into Martin Buser, a winner of the Alaskan Iditarod Trail sled dog race, and his pack was a textbook lesson in teamwork, efficiency, and alignment. But it is not always that way. Huskies are very aggressive. The wolf genes are not far below the surface, and when packs fight, the raw aggression and violence come boiling to the surface.

Different communication styles work in different situations. In mushing, the idea of the alpha dog never applies more clearly, and a musher's communication style needs to reflect this. It is essential to have one big dog in charge, or else the pack descends into chaos – something like the "storming stage" of power struggles and role clarification in team development. The pack needs to know who the lead dog is. When mushing, you need to be the alpha dog. Sometimes at work, you will need to be the director.

To gain control over the dogs, the instructors told us to make our commands clear, confident, and crisp. *Hike* meant go, *gee* meant turn right, *haw* meant turn left, *easy* meant slow, and *whoa* meant stop. The dogs came together very quickly under my commands, but the other instructors

(cont'd)

seemed to struggle to get the dogs to work together. The dogs would snap and snarl at each other, were slow to turn when commanded, and were constantly fighting with each other.

I pondered how I had been able to get the team under control so quickly when the other mushers struggled with the same dogs. I had studied some psychology and knew some principles of how to use reward and punishment. That had to be it, I reasoned. If the team made an error, I was quick to correct it. I refused to accept any deviation from the desired route, and I crushed anything that looked like emerging dissent. I immodestly complimented myself on my thorough and effective application of psychological principles – until I discovered that the dogs had come from the Australian Antarctic Territory. Having been trained by Aussies handlers, they had learned to respond quickly and obediently to an Australian accent!

When it comes to how to treat your team members at work, you should obviously not view them or treat them like sled dogs. It does, however, make a difference what language you speak when you mush your team. And in some situations, alignment comes when you take a very clear directing-style role.

One of the barriers to getting things done is the inability to speak more than one language. I am not referring to Spanish, Portuguese, or Mandarin, but rather the different languages spoken by each of the functional disciplines and the different levels of the organization. There is a need for more multilingual speakers and translators. More than one company has a separate website for nothing but TLAs (three-letter acronyms). Our functional languages help us with precision when talking to peers within our areas of expertise but get in the way when talking across functions.

When talking upwards, executives may feel that senior managers don't hear their concerns unless they use the language of the boardroom. Individual contributors may not connect with their boss if their language doesn't reflect a concern for broader issues than their immediate technical focus, no matter how important the issue, or how well reasoned it is.

How many languages can you speak? Here are some tips for speaking more languages:

- *Use BusinessDictionary.com to build your business vocabulary*
- *Learn how to read a shareholder's report.*
- *Create a rule for cross-functional meetings that any acronyms used must be explained.*
- *Start a collection of stories to appeal to different audiences that illustrates your core values, beliefs, etc.*

As part of your teambuilding efforts, share your communication preferences. Some people prefer data leading up to a conclusion; others prefer the conclusion first and will explore the data if they want to dive deeper. Some people prefer information in sentences; others prefer it in bullet form. Some are persuaded by stories, others by a strong presentation of numerical data. Adjusting your communication style to others' preferences can help you get your message across. I-Speak is one assessment tool to start a conversation around communication style preferences, or help you flex your style.

Avoid Ladders of Assumptions

A large splatter of rust-covered blood filled the view through my goggles as I inched my way across a rickety aluminum ladder. The ladder stretched across a 170-foot-deep crevasse on Everest's lower slopes. It was a double ladder; two had been lashed together end on end, so it was particularly tenuous, even with the safety lines attached that were intended to catch us climbers if we fell. There was no way to avoid the visual impact, and it was a wake-up call to the risks our group faced as we moved up the mountain.

I don't know all the details, but I learned later that a Sherpa, who had not clipped into the safety lines, had fallen into the crevasse and died. Sherpas sometimes skip clipping in to save time. They can carry more loads and earn more money that way. Perhaps it was overconfidence on the Sherpa's part. Either way, for me it was a very sad but focusing moment.

The consequences are not always as terrible as they were in the story above, but ladders of assumptions create delays and have big costs in organizations as well.

As leaders, we have a limited pool of observable data and experience. From that pool, we select certain data and experiences to pay attention to, and then we affix meaning to that. Based on the meaning we attach to the data, we make assumptions, draw conclusions, create beliefs about people or the environment, and then take actions. The beliefs we create shape the data we select the next time.

How do you avoid making unwarranted assumptions? *Actively seek out data that may be contrary to your experiences or beliefs. Use a devil's advocate in decision making; invite others with different viewpoints, make your own assumptions overt, and test them.*

Context

Sometimes it's not just what you say but the setting in which you say it that determines how a message is received and interpreted. Location, history, and prior relationships all shape how messages are received. Not understanding this almost led to a drowning incident – mine.

I was on a three-week diving expedition on the Great Barrier Reef with the Institute of Marine Science. It was one of those days that seemed too beautiful for anything bad to happen, but it did. Most of us had just earned our entry-level Open Water Diver certificates. We were all keen to master the skills and progressively more challenging dives, so we spent our spare hours flashing hand signals to each other and practicing communication as though we were underwater.

We packed a boat full of fresh tanks of air, weight belts, and the rest of our diving paraphernalia, and headed out. You always dive with a partner in case anything goes wrong, so we picked a diving buddy on the way out. We rigged up, flipped over the side of the boat, and drifted downwards with just our air bubbles breaking the silence. **(cont'd)**

141

John, my diving buddy, and I cruised along the bottom at 90 feet with no worries. As we got more confident, we started drifting apart. We were off in our own worlds, both figuratively and literally.

Then my tank started dragging, and it was getting harder and harder to pull the air from the tank into my lungs. Although I did not realize it at the time, the air gauge that I had picked up was faulty. I was about to run out of air, and I was 90 feet underwater.

The first thing they taught us in SCUBA training was DON'T PANIC (it is always written in caps in the diver training manuals). I swam calmly over to John and made the signals for "out of air" and "I want to buddy-breathe" as calmly as I could. (This was before the days of dual breathing regulators.) Apparently, because I did it so calmly, he thought I was still practicing my signals, so he waved at me and swam off chasing some marine life. Oh, S…

Since John was my nearest source of oxygen, I swam calmly over to him again and made the signals for "out of air" and "I want to buddy-breathe" – as calmly as I could. Again he waved at me and swam off, obviously still thinking I was merely practicing my communication signals.

After unsuccessfully trying to communicate with John again, I decided to do a free ascent to the surface with the little air that remained in my tank. Going too fast, I would risk getting the bends – decompression sickness. Going too slow could mean running short of air. When I broke the surface, I had half a gulp of air left. You can imagine that my communication was fairly clear and direct when I caught up with my dive buddy!

One lesson that stands out is that the context in which a message is being sent and received impacts the way the actual content of the message is interpreted. The history of prior communications, the setting, and the relationship all impact how our messages are received. The context here was that we were practicing our communication signals, and my lack of visible signs of panic reinforced the sense of any lack of danger. The benign sea conditions and sunny weather may also have contributed to a sense that this was a safe context.

As an example, why is it that many of us cringe when people ask if they can give us some feedback? Feedback could be comments we interpret as either positive or negative. Many of us associate feedback with awkward performance appraisals. The setting may have been someone else's office (their power center) that we have been summoned to, and the relationship, at least during the performance appraisal, may have an adult/child dynamic where we are there to receive or not receive their approval.

One of my failures as a leader occurred when I forgot the context lesson, specifically the importance of history. I had come into a new nonprofit organization as a director. I was full of zeal and had ideas that I thought were creative, synergistic, and going to help everyone. I envisioned win-wins all around. I seemed to have strong buy-in from the board and the executive director. What I missed by failing to delve deeply enough into the history of the organization was that the executive director had made a number of promises that were now unwritten expectations. My ideas countered those expectations, so I was met with silent, passive resistance. My initiatives floundered, and after nine months, it was suggested that maybe there was a better fit for my ideas in another organization. Some of my lessons learned were:

Assessing an organization effectively prior to making changes requires a full timeline perspective – past, present, and future. Ask questions to understand others' perspectives through all three lenses.

When analyzing stakeholders' interests, the perspectives of those responsible for executing the vision are just as important as stakeholders creating the vision. Passive resistance probably kills more change initiatives than outright opposition.

Create a guiding coalition that includes both strategy and execution perspectives. Don't assume everyone shares your needs. Change is likely to create shifts in status, resources, and probably authority. Ask: "Who will win and who will lose what?" Consider what can you do to offset any losses with other compensations, appeals to the greater good, use of formal authority if absolutely necessary, or some other strategy.

When you communicate with others, what history or context might you be missing? How are you going to uncover that? You might ask people to tell you a story that highlights an important event, value, person, or issue that helped the organization to get to where it is today. You might ask people about the tensions and challenges between values that the organization has wrestled with over the years and how those have been resolved or not. You could ask people when the organization was at its best and what has been lost or gained since.

How can you avoid misreading the situation like John, my SCUBA buddy, did? Asking people to paraphrase what they heard rather than just indicating whether they understood you can be very helpful. Having an alternative communications medium sometimes helps a message get through differently. If I had been carrying an underwater slate, I could have sent a different message and shifted the context, possibly reducing the risk of misinterpretation.

How can you avoid sending signals that might be misinterpreted because of the context, as I did in my organizational change story? One approach, especially if you are new to a situation, is to create an anonymous or group setting in which people can raise issues with less fear. To avoid setting an inappropriate precedent, I would also say something like "Eventually, I'd like us to be able to be really candid with each other, but I realize it will take a while to build that comfort level." Facilitation tools like a Force Field Analysis or Scenario Development can provide objectivity and provide permission to challenge a leader's thinking.

Speak Up/Listen Up

In an attempt to improve communications, many companies have created campaigns to encourage their employees to speak up. They have had varying degrees of success. BP is one of the companies that have done so. Bob Dudley, the CEO of BP, adopted "Speak Up" as one of his mantras. Not too long after launching this campaign, however, BP leaders began commenting on the importance of their own "listening up" to support employees in speaking up.

Research across corporations suggests two main reasons that people do not speak up. Fear of reprisals, which can range from losing one's job to being cut out of social or communication loops, is one of the reasons. The other is the feeling that nothing will change. Steps you can take to help include:

- *Being ruthless in rooting out any retaliation for speaking up.*
- *Positively rewarding people who speak up.*
- *Completing the loop. (Keep a log of suggestions and requests that your team members bring up.)*
- *Using a consultative style where appropriate, and when decisions are made, let team members and stakeholders know the rationale behind them.*
- *Sharing stories about how speaking up contributed to a positive change.*

Whom Do You Listen To?

Most organizations are complex, noisy places. As an individual, there are many voices vying for your attention – kids, employers, charity groups, the media, schools, and relatives, for example. It is very easy to react to the loudest and most strident voices. The challenge is "hearing the quietest voice in the room," as Bob Dudley puts it. Sometimes, the quietest voices are unheard because they are drowned out. Sometimes they are unheard because they are thinking more deeply, and sometimes they are putting others' needs first. It takes an active, sustained effort to create a team or organization that seeks out the quietest voice in the room.

Telling people, before a meeting what input you are seeking, Brainwriting, anonymous polling, and assigning time blocks for each meeting participant are examples of facilitation tools you can use to bring quieter voices into the room.

145

The Maze is the name that outdoors instructors at Joshua Tree gave to an area of several square miles of winding canyons and jumbled boulders the size of houses piled on top of each other. It is very tricky terrain. My fellow instructors and I took groups into this area to investigate lessons in dealing with ambiguity and to help people explore their responses to getting lost, a life metaphor with wide applications.

Tony Robbins points out that we need both certainty and uncertainty in our lives.[42] Too much uncertainty stops us from moving forward; too much certainty can lead us into dangerous places, literally and figuratively. Too much certainty in navigation can create a situation where we fit the map to the ground – we see things how we want to see them, not as they really are. Leaders, once convinced of their own picture, tend to bias towards the positive, and they can sometimes ignore those who bring them the reality. They screen out data that doesn't confirm their map. I know; I have done it.

We all have our own map of the terrain. As a leader and navigator, your role is to gather those diverse perspectives to create a more accurate view of the landscape. If there is a cliff on your path, you need to know about it in order to help the team find a way around it.

My facilitator colleagues and I once guided a group of hard-charging, gung-ho managers (11 men and one woman) from a retail company through The Maze in Joshua Tree. The leaders of this company were known for their aggressive business strategy and confident attitude. One element of their strategy included swamping a new geographic market with stores so that the competition could not get a foothold. Cannibalizing their own stores' territory was considered an acceptable loss in their efforts to dominate market share.

(cont'd)

---

[42]   Robbins, A. (1996). *Personal Power.* [Audiobook]. San Diego, CA: Robbins Research International.

Once into The Maze, we told the team that they would be responsible for navigating us through to the other side. After a surprisingly quick huddle, the team headed off into the jumble of boulders. They proceeded to get lost, although they believed they knew where they were. The terrain restricted their view, and the height of the cliffs distorted their perspective. Their overconfidence, perhaps an asset in other situations, became a liability as they tried to force the map to conform to their image of the terrain.

The reality on the ground, however, gradually made them realize that they were not where they thought they were. Unfortunately, their response was to push even harder. Their plan was to go over the top of a series of high rock outcrops that they believed was standing in their way, so the other instructors and I stepped in. As much as we applauded their willingness to face the challenges, they were not equipped for what they were proposing, and we were not willing to compromise their safety.

When we imposed a pause to check the map, the sole woman finally found her voice. She had been questioning their direction all along, but her voice had been drowned out. Part of her silence was because she was paying the most attention to the map and terrain. The route she now proposed, although less direct, was relatively straightforward, and the group was able to exit The Maze safely with far less effort. Her credibility with the group rose.

Some of the lessons to be learned from this story are:

Listen to the quietest voice.

The quietest voice in the room may be the most thoughtful.

Provide a variety of methods for communicating ideas.

A voice does not have to be verbal. Some team members might contribute more effectively by communicating their thoughts in writing either before or after a meeting.

Coach deeper and more thoughtful thinkers on how, and when, to speak up.

One tactic is to have these employees raise an issue in a meeting, but ask for permission to explore it in more depth and get back to the team. This tactic simultaneously builds their visibility and utilizes their preferred working style.

Create procedures in advance to manage both overconfidence and lack of certainty.

These might include, for example, a team rule that if someone is uncertain about a safety, they can stop work; a rotating role for a black hat (pessimistic) thinker; guard against sunk cost by periodically asking: "If we were to start this project again, would we? Would we do it the same way?"

Check the culture.

Culture (what gets rewarded, values, stories, and artifacts) impacts the patterns of communication – what gets discussed, who is allowed to raise it, and who is effectively heard. Use data from cultural surveys and your own observations to examine how the culture is shaping communication in your organization. In some cases, it may make sense to gather outsiders' perspectives.

What are you doing as a leader to create the right balance between confidence and uncertainty?

Who has the quietest voice on your team, in your family, or in your community group? What are you doing to ensure you hear that voice?

Here are some small steps for strengthening general communication.

Small Steps

1. *Clarify your intent before engaging in a conversation. Is it to communicate a message, influence someone to do something differently, or understand someone else's position?*

2. *Observe and seek feedback on whether your impact matched your intent.*

3. *Don't bury the headline. Rather than building up to your headline, offer it first. Then explain your rationale if asked for more details.*

4. *Highlight what is important. Create space around your core concepts to help them stand out. When you speak, avoid run-on sentences. Insert pauses before and after key points. In an email, use spacing, paragraphs, texts, headlines, and sub-headlines to do this.*

5. *Check your balance. How much are you communicating (top-down, informing, telling) versus engaging with people (multi-directional dialog, including emotional content, asking questions)?*

CHAPTER 9
Energy Management

"Managing Energy, Not Time, Is the Key to High Performance."

– Jim Loehr and Tony Schwartz, *The Power of Full Engagement*

Too many companies fail to sustain a long life because they burn out in one way or another. Too many employees also burn out or become disengaged. This chapter explores some energy-management lessons from the outdoors and professional athletes.

Organizations such as SportsMind, the Human Performance Institute (HPI), and various national sporting bodies have researched athletes' approaches to energy management and performance. What can their research tell us about improving performance and effectiveness in a work context?

Types of Energy

According to these organizations, and based on my experiences, athletes with longer, more successful careers manage a number of different types of energy, which are described as physical, emotional, interpersonal, mental, relational, and spiritual. Terms associated with mental energy are innovation, conceptualization, cognitive learning, process management, mental flexibility, creativity, and agility. Relational energy refers to the breadth and depth of a person's relationships. Physical energy refers to factors such as diet and nutrition, health, fitness, strength, hydration, and sleep. Emotional energy refers to the depth and range of emotions a person experiences and that person's capacity for harnessing these emotions to achieve a goal. Interpersonal energy is energy either withheld or released as a result of interactions between team members. Spiritual energy is derived from clarity of purpose and alignment between the other energy dimensions.

151

Alison Levine was the team leader of the first American Women's Everest Expedition. She describes a very different energy in the teams of her 2002 and 2010 expeditions, which she attributes to differences in selection processes, "performance ego," and "team ego."[43]

Spiritual energy represents a sense of purpose, meaningful work, or sense of calling beyond just making a profit. Some organizations, consciously or unconsciously, attempt to tap into this energy through their vision, mission, or corporate citizenship activities.

Modern scientific research validates ancient wisdom regarding the interrelationship between different forms of energy. Buddha said: "Inward calm cannot be maintained unless physical strength is constantly and intelligently replenished," while the prophet Isaiah claimed: "those who hope in the LORD will renew their strength. They will soar on wings like eagles; they will run and not grow weary, they will walk and not be faint" (Isaiah 40:31, New International Version).

Energy management has implications at the organizational development level, not just the personal development level. Two high-performance energies, mental and interpersonal, can be characterized as initiating energies, and three others, physical, emotional, and spiritual, can be described as sustaining energies.

One question that usually gets laughs in big corporations is: What is your organization better at: initiating change or sustaining change? Sports performance research may partially explain why most organizations struggle with sustaining change. Almost all of their energy goes into conceptualizing the change and communicating it to stakeholders. They direct far less energy into examining the emotional impacts the changes have on individuals, or the physical energy people need to keep pushing the change forward and take on additional work requirements.

---

43   Levine, A. (2014). *On the Edge: The Art of High-Impact Leadership* (Unabridged. ed.). New York, NY: Grand Central Publishing.

To embed change, ensure that you help people manage the sustaining energies (physical, emotional, spiritual).

Taking a more holistic approach to engaging people helps people manage their energy. Organizations experience lower levels of disengagement when they allow employees to bring more of themselves to work. "Aligning energy investments with one's deepest values and beliefs represents a critical component to skillful energy management."[44]

When our bodies are out of alignment, it responds with pain or finds ways to protect itself. Individuals who are out of alignment with their own or an organization's values, goals, or methods often respond by disengaging or trying to conserve their energy. Organizations take on similar coping strategies. These coping strategies often show up as resistance to change, divergence in leadership direction, or dilution of the vision.

Motivation and Engagement

Let's look at some examples of different kinds of energy and the link to motivation and engagement. We tend to think of motivation as something leaders do to followers. To prevent leaders from burning out, it would be better to think of energy as something leaders and followers exchange. We all have our energy low points, but it is less common for everyone to be at a low point at the same time. We all have reserves that few of us tap into except in emergencies. As team members and leaders, we can help each other exchange and tap into those energy reserves.

Like the Canada geese, we can support each other by honking from behind. Good followership supports those in a leadership role. Leaders gain good followership by investing emotionally and relationally in their people.

---

[44] *The Corporate Athlete® Course.* (n.d.). Retrieved January 21, 2016, from https://www.jjhpi.com/training-solutions/corporate-athlete

My mates in the Army frequently helped me go beyond what I perceived to be my physical limits, for example, when I represented my company in a 5,000-meter steeplechase race. I was sick and only got two hours sleep the night before the race. That morning, I had to get all my vaccine shots. They made me woozy, and I needed some calories, so I crammed down four Mars bars about 90 minutes before the race started. I was a mess physically, but I didn't feel like I could pull out of the race and let down the team.

My memory of the race is very foggy beyond the first lap, and I counted one of the laps three times. My brain was not functioning, my legs were turning over but felt like jelly, and the race seemed to go on forever. Even worse was the fact that I was running last. The potential embarrassment of having our company coming last terrified me, so I poured everything I had into the final lap. I needed at least to catch the person who was 15 yards in front of me. The company was cheering for me, which raised my spirits and encouraged me further. I clawed in the distance between us as I poured on the pace on the final straight. It looked like I might catch him – until my legs gave way beneath me.

My mates told me that I collapsed four times on the final straight. Two runners passed me while I was getting back on my feet, and I was horrified that I had been lapped – the ultimate humiliation for any runner. What got me back on my feet was not my personal drive, but rather the energy of the crowd. My final collapse was into the arms of a paramedic as I crossed the finish line. I was devastated and humiliated. It puzzled me that people had been cheering for such a miserable performance.

It turned out, though, that I had been running second and was just about to catch the winner when I crashed to the ground for the first time. The two runners who passed me had not lapped me. I had finished fourth.

(cont'd)

After the race, I spent a few days in the hospital recovering from dehydration. It would have been easy to feel sorry for myself except that my mates kept dropping in to visit. My race experience, along with the support they gave me during and afterward, encouraged me through other future challenges.

The experience still provides me with muscle memory that tells me when I am reaching the end of my endurance physically. In the mountains, it has enabled me to push on when I know that the environment is relatively safe and turn back when running out of reserves would be dangerous.

We can also apply the energy-exchange principle to mental or relational energy. We can take in energy from others when our reserves are low. During my race, relational energy (my company's support for me) and emotional energy (joy at competing and the crowd's energy) helped shore up my will when my physical reserves were low.

Have you put enough energy into connecting with your team, colleagues, and managers on a relational and emotional level, or has it all gone into the mental aspects of task completion? Do you have people around you who will give you energy back when you need it, or are you assuming you have to do everything on your own? Ask others to be cheerleaders for you. Let them know how best to cheer for you and be sensitive to what is appropriate in your organizational culture. Do you view business as a sprint or a marathon?

Too many people burn themselves out because they do not maintain an adequate reserve for unexpected challenges. At times, corporate athletes need to be able to sprint to meet deadlines, but they more often need endurance on a day-to-day basis.

You can play a part in leading a team by monitoring your energy, but also by looking for ways to pass along energy to others. Is a colleague stuck mentally? Maybe you can offer a fresh perspective on a problem. Has a new team member joined your group? Reach out and build a relational connection.

Help release employees' mental energy by emphasizing what needs to be accomplished and avoiding unnecessary restrictions on how they do it.

The organizational benefits of helping employees release their mental energy goes beyond the short-term benefits of task efficiency, though. It increases engagement, innovation, and development of judgment, problem-solving skills, and succession-readiness.

Mental energy receives a lot of focus in organizations, and most people recognize the importance of investing in relationships for the purpose of getting things done. Emotional energy, on the other hand, is something that we tend to neglect. Rather than discussing it, the attitude is more often that people should "suck it up" or "deal with it."

The people who I have found to be most impressive when it comes to managing energy are also often the poorest in terms of financial resources. The guides and porters in places like Tanzania, Indonesia, Bolivia, Nepal, and Ecuador often have poor diets, no fancy gym memberships for training, or psychologists to help them when they have relational problems. And yet they find ways to support each other in tough, physical lives through close personal relationships and by rituals and celebration of what we might consider the most trivial of things. We may not often think about our responsibilities to each other in terms of helping each other manage energy, but there are significant lessons we can learn from the guides and porters I just mentioned.

The Annapurna Circuit in Nepal in 1978 was an amazing trek with rope ladders swinging across rushing rivers, Buddhist flags fluttering in the wind, and sometimes thousands of feet to climb and descend a day. The year I was there for a 22-day expedition with seven others was the second year it was open to Westerners after having been closed for 35 years. At the time, it was the 10th poorest nation in the world. There were minimal facilities and no Internet or cell phones. The only Western thing we came across was Coca-Cola. On the trail today, though, there are many Western-style hotels and amenities, and a road is being pushed along one of the major valleys. **(cont'd)**

We went local for our trip, eating dhal bhat tarkari (lentils, rice, and fried vegetables) and chapattis and drinking endless cups of tea each day. The porters got up before dawn to start fires and bring tea to us, and then they carried up to 120 pounds on their backs all day. Still, they found the energy to celebrate, sing, and dance late into the evening.

The feet that carried the cups of steaming tea to wake us in the morning were often barefoot, even in snow, because they were trying not to wear out the cheap shoes we bought them. Due to poverty, the porters typically got just a few meat meals per year. One evening, we decided to purchase a couple of chickens to add to the staple dinner of dhal bhat tarkari. We camped high on a very narrow ridge that night. After the tents were up, the porters invited us to watch the "beheading of the chickens," an event preceded by much anticipation and ceremony.

Some of our porters had been Gurkhas, who have a proud soldiering tradition. Once their wicked-looking Kukri knives are drawn from their sheaths, custom dictates that the knives must draw blood.

The Kukris came out, flashed in the dying sun, and swiftly and cleanly sliced through the chickens' necks. Unfortunately, the chickens, without their heads, took off down the side of the mountain. After the porters exchanged a few quick glances, they took off *en masse* down the side of the mountain chasing the headless chickens. Rocks, bodies, and chickens went flying in every direction, but eventually, the escapees were apprehended. The porters came back up over the cliff edge with massive grins, laughing uproariously. It seemed like the rakshi (rice-wine)-fueled celebrations were even more boisterous than usual that night.

The porters' capacity to find the joy in simple things, even when surrounded by grinding poverty and hardship, constantly amazes me. Why do we so rarely take the time to celebrate small wins and be grateful for even the small things we do have? How can we create a culture of celebration?

- *Build in quick celebration points to mark milestones.*

157

- *Since the synergy of the team is greater than the sum of the individual contributions, recognize people for their unique contributions to the team, not just how many widgets they produce.*
- *Establish rituals that build a human connection through shared memories and experiences.*
- *Start a personal gratitude journal and make it one of the first and last things you do in your day.*
- *During team development sessions, ask people about what they are proud of in their family, community, or team.*

Energy Exchange

You can clearly see and feel an energy exchange when someone is presenting. The audience usually returns energy to presenters who invest energy in their audience.

I once had a temporary job as a traveling dinosaur lecturer. I traveled around outback Queensland and down the tropical rainforest coast towing a trailer filled with an inflatable life-size Tyrannosaurus Rex and a collection of dinosaur fossils in large glass cases – Stegosaurus plates, Tyrannosaurus skulls, Velociraptor claws, and fossilized dinosaur dung. For the most part, I stopped at small elementary schools that were many miles from anywhere. My lectures were the most novel thing that happened all year in some of those towns. I was featured on the front page of local newspapers. It was a fun job; I would do a few hours of presentations a day and then drive a couple of hundred miles to the next town and spend the rest of the day hiking, caving, surfing, or sightseeing.

The kids would wait eagerly for months for "The Dinosaur Man." As I would pull into the playground and start inflating the life-size T. Rex, they would go crazy. Typically, about 40 to 100 children and one or two very nervous teachers attended. Dinosaurs seem to attract an intense emotional energy from children. Even if my energy were low, the kids would immediately lift

(cont'd)

me up with their enthusiasm. How can children of such a young age learn how to pronounce those ridiculously long, multisyllabic dinosaur names or memorize the details of dozens of species? The topic itself is one of great interest to kids of that age, but when emotional energy supports it, it dramatically reinforces the mental energy and cognitive recall.

For my part, I tried to inject energy through moments of whispered tones, silence, building expectations, and crescendos of emotional release. I received much more than I gave during these times. Driving the engagement of the audience by asking questions, having competitions, bringing children up on stage, letting them handle the fossils, and putting them into the stories helped create and harness energy in this scenario.

How can you engage with your audience rather than just presenting something to them?

Do you know what your employees are most passionate about? Are you finding ways to integrate and align their passions into your presentations? How do you want people to think, feel, and do things differently when you have finished? Have you considered using a presentation coach to help you master the energy exchange between you and your audiences?

Peak Teams is one organization that does a masterful job of harnessing an audience's energy to support alignment efforts in big change initiatives. Their presenters bring inspiration, and their facilitation processes tap into the energy of the audience members to drive true engagement. Inspirations light the flame; engagement keeps it going. Some of the techniques I learned from them for harnessing an audience's energy are:

- Mix with the audience before you start to build a few connections.
- Focus on your intent, even before the content. How do you want people to think, feel, or act differently?
- Start with a provocative question. Get people actively involved early on.

- Get people moving. Ask people to stand up for something they agree with. Use lineups on the ground to illustrate movement towards or away from a viewpoint as proposals are made. Ask people to cluster around issues listed on flipcharts that they have the most energy around.
- Get people engaged with each other, not the main speaker. Have people discuss an issue in pairs or threes before reporting out to the larger audience.

Energy Drains

Fear is a major energy drain in both outdoor pursuits and the workplace. Fear drains physical energy, but it also impacts mental clarity. It damages relationships between people and can set up vicious cycles impacting emotions and performance.

As a beginning rock climber, I made most of the classic rookie mistakes. I gripped the rock too tightly, thereby draining my finger strength. (New managers have a tendency to take too much control.) I leaned into and hugged the rock, thinking that it would give me additional security, but all that did was force me out of balance and restrict my vision to what was immediately in front of me. Then my world and options shrunk. (New managers tend to cling to what they know best rather than lean back and take in a bigger view.) I rushed my moves, thinking I would run out of energy rather than thinking about how to conserve my energy through smooth, controlled moves. (New leaders often struggle to find the pacing that meets their manager's needs while not wearing out their team.)

Ways to manage energy and maximize performance. Here are some ideas on how you, your team, and your organization can manage your energy and maximize your performance:

Kill the energy vampires. Exploring a meandering limestone cave passage, I entered a very tight squeeze with only a few inches of wiggle room. So when dozens of bats started pouring through the passage, they tangled in my hair, clothes, and mouth. Apparently, they felt like they were under threat, and I was blocking their escape route. We often fail to see the small events that continually drain our energy. Jim Loehr, a performance psychologist, calls these energy vampires.

One of the sad facts of search and rescue is that people are often found in very poor shape because they have not managed their energy. Protective gear lies unused in their backpacks. Clothing is not zipped up. They fail to protect themselves from exposure to wind, cold, or rain. The crisis they are in reduces their mental capacity. For this reason, they are not aware of the energy that leaks out and the actions they could have taken to improve their situation.

Loehr recommends doing an audit of the things that drain your energy, evaluate how important these things are, and eliminate as many of them as you can.

Organizations have energy vampires too, such as rework due to misaligned goals, unproductive meetings, and unnecessary paperwork. Do a little exploring, shine your flashlight in the darkness, and call the vampires out into the light.

Consider having someone outside your group do a culture audit to provide an outside perspective.

Work teams can borrow a group management technique from hikers and mountaineers. Hypothermia is hard to spot when it impacts you, so team members are tasked with watching for the "umbles" in each other. The umbles are stumbles, mumbles, grumbles, fumbles – indicators that team members are losing energy and that their body temperature is dropping too low. If the team detects the umbles in someone, they take action to help that individual regain energy through shelter, hot drinks, energy food, or other means.

Monitor your team's energy. Are there people on your team who are showing the umbles? What can you do to help them restore their energy?

Emphasize capability building over coping. Athletes with long, successful careers emphasize long-term capability building strategies over short-term coping mechanisms. Coffee, Red Bull, and pulling an all-nighter are coping strategies. Learning effective conflict management skills, exercising regularly, and having a support network are tools to build capability.

Big-wave surfers frequently build their lung capacity by running under water with large rocks. That capacity can be lifesaving if they are caught in a "hold-down" situation where several big waves crash over them in rapid succession. (Carlos Burle has the record for the largest wave ridden – a 100-footer off Portugal.)

Throwing more money, time, or people at a problem is also a coping strategy. Improving alignment, engagement, and processes are capability-building activities.

Improve processes before adding resources.

In the mountains, I carry Gu Energy shots in case I need more physical energy, but it is the cardio, mobility, and strength training in the months ahead that I rely on for the most part.

Coping strategies have their place. Like 98% of those who climb Mount Everest, I used oxygen at the highest levels of the mountain. The most impressive athletes climb without it, albeit with greatly increased risks. Running out of oxygen can put you in a serious position. On Everest, I passed the body of one climber who died, presumably of exhaustion, after running out of oxygen. She had used 13 bottles; we had used two. Sometimes the answer is not just more resources.

Coping strategies are short-term fixes, though. Overuse often causes an eventual decline in performance at the individual, team, and organizational levels. Some types of restructuring efforts are still widely used by organizations to improve financial performance, in spite of overwhelming research that suggests that they provide only short-term benefits. Fewer organizations successfully address the culture and strategy challenges at work that led them to be less competitive.

Too many of us rely too often on coping strategies rather than investing in increasing our abilities to take on more significant challenges and handle the associated pressure.

How much of your week did you spend building capability versus relying on coping strategies?

Jim Loehr suggests several ways to build capability:

1. Because energy capacity diminishes both with overuse and with underuse, we must balance energy expenditure with intermittent energy renewal.

2. [P]ush beyond our normal limits, training in the same systematic way that elite athletes do.

3. [Create] positive energy rituals – highly specific routines for managing energy. This is the key to full engagement and sustained high performance.[45]

Build rituals into daily, quarterly, and annual meetings.

Use your strengths. In their book *Strengths Based Leadership,* Tom Rath and Barry Conchie suggest that employees are much more engaged when their work frequently calls on their natural talents.[46] Talents need to be exercised through stretch assignments, reflective learning, and feedback to develop them into strengths.

---

[45]   Loehr, J.E. (1994). *The New Toughness Training for Sports: Mental, Emotional, and Physical Conditioning from One of the World's Premier Sports Psychologists.* New York, NY: Plume.

[46]   Rath, T., & Conchie, B. (2008). *Strengths Based Leadership: Great Leaders, Teams, and Why People Follow.* New York, NY: Gallup Press.

Ask your team members to read Strengths Based Leadership *and set up a discussion with you about how you can best help them leverage their strengths.*

Even great athletes have relative weaknesses. A strengths-based approach suggests four main ways to address weakness. Three of these require less energy, which can then be reinvested in leveraging strengths. Development through feedback and coaching is one option. Delegation, directly or by outsourcing, is a second option. Designing a process such as a checklist is a third option. Deploying into a different job is a fourth option.

Fun and Play

According to a William M. Mercer survey, only 29 percent of employers nationwide encourage humor as part of their company culture, and only eight percent have a policy of using fun to reduce employee stress. Yet, research at California State University Long Beach showed that people who have fun at work are more creative, more productive, work better with others and call in sick less often.[47]

A good starting point for introducing more fun into the workplace is to examine your attitude to work and challenges. In *Born to Run*, Christopher McDougall contrasts the Western approach to long-distance running, which we call endurance and see more as an individual event, with the far more playful and relational approach of the Tarahumara Indians who live in a remote area of Mexico.[48] Perhaps because they live in widely dispersed settlements, they seem to have made the most of what one could otherwise perceive as an onerous task – travel. The men regularly run in relays, kicking a wooden ball, and the women run with a stick and hoop – up to 200 miles in a single session. Competitions can be called at a moment's notice and are often preceded by heavy celebratory drinking of the locally produced alcohol.

47   Stern, T. (2007, February 16). *Ten Ways to Inject Fun into the Workplace.* Retrieved May 13, 2015, from http://www.fastcompany.com/659698/ten-ways-inject-fun-workplace

48   McDougall, C. (2009). *Born to Run: A Hidden Tribe, Superathletes, and the Greatest Race the Word Has Never Seen.* New York, NY: Random House.

For many people, fun means doing meaningful work, work that they are intrinsically motivated by. Google encourages employees to invest time in their projects of interest, and they free up their employees' time to do so.

Do you know what fun and play mean to your people? Is it getting together socially, brainstorming new ideas, intellectual exploration of new ideas, office pranks, or something else? How are you encouraging your team to help build fun and play into the daily routine?

CHAPTER 10

Dealing With Storms

Business storms come in many forms, and they can range from an inconvenient headwind to a destructive hurricane. Examples include:

- A breach of IT security
- Turnover of key staff
- An industrial accident
- Labor disputes
- Changes in legislation
- Disruptions in distribution or supply
- Product recalls

The ability to weather a storm is not just a survival issue but also a potential competitive advantage. In the airlines storm immediately following 9/11, many airlines adopted a "hunker down" strategy, scaling back operations and laying off employees. That strategy did not stop the red ink and led to big drops in customer satisfaction and morale, making recovery even more challenging. Southwest Airlines had the capacity to fly directly through the storm (maybe not the best flying metaphor!) retaining all their employees and announcing a profit-sharing scheme. They were able to do that because they were resourced adequately before the storm. Southwest still has an unbroken record of yearly profitability.

Storms are inevitable on big mountains and in any industry. Knowing when you can push through and when to hunker down comes through watching the weather, experience, training, and having the right reserve resources.

Having an effective crisis management plan will help reduce the impact of storms, even if you can't move out of their way. Crisis management plans should combine both control-oriented and adaptive approaches. One framework incorporates four stages: anticipation and preparation, crisis analysis, response, and recovery. This chapter looks at some internally and externally generated crises and what we can learn from adventurers' strategies for coping with them.

Anticipation and Preparation

Anticipation starts with risk assessment. Backcountry skiers use a variety of methods to assess avalanche risk, including terrain analysis and scanning the environment for potential triggers. They may change the route of travel, carry rescue beacons, or cancel a trip depending on the severity and location of the risks.

Risks can come from the external environment or inside an organization. Organizations can use tools like scenario planning or the PEST (Political, Economic, Social, Technological) framework to come up with avoidance and mitigation strategies.

On a sailing expedition along the Alaskan coast, our crew had to steer well clear of icebergs, since there is far more mass below the surface than above, and they have been known to tip over occasionally.

Risk assessments should include organizational factors that exist below the waterline, such as culture and unwritten rules, not just what you can see above the surface.

Watch for environmental signals. People have long observed animal behavior for signs of changing environmental conditions.

The day before the Landers earthquake in California, I was hiking nearby in Joshua Tree National Park. I saw nine rattlesnakes in one afternoon, which was more than I had seen in multiple seasons. They were not only more obvious but also more active and aggressive than usual. In training classes for my pilot's license, I learned to recognize cloud sequences that indicated shifting weather patterns and changing flight risks. I later used that knowledge when mountaineering, thereby reducing my reliance on more generalized forecasts.

168

What patterns have historically led to storms in your industry? Is the climate changing in ways that might indicate the emergence of new or more significant threats?

Preplanning includes strategies such as prepositioning equipment for faster response (a lesson relearned after Hurricane Katrina) and mock tabletop or field simulation exercises. These often point out underlying weaknesses in an organizations' ability to respond effectively.

A colleague worked with organizations responsible for responding to the London transport bombings of 2005. The First Responder teams, according to him, performed much better than management, partly because they had more frequent training but also because they had greater clarity of focus. The First Responders focused on serving one stakeholder group (victims). The managers struggled to deal with other departments, the media, the government, and numerous other stakeholder groups.

Training and leveraging experience are common preparation strategies. It is particularly helpful for infrequent but high consequence risks and is most valuable when it teaches transferable skills to help manage rogue and unanticipated crises.

For one of my birthdays, I went tandem skydiving. Before we jumped from 14,000 feet, the instructor put me through a number of training drills to address potential chute malfunctions. The training turned out to be a good thing. Launching out of the aircraft, we went into the standard arch position to stabilize, and I started to enjoy the adrenaline rush of a long freefall. But I was surprised to hear my instructor scream, "Arch!" again. The main chute had not deployed correctly, so he had made the decision to cut it away and go to the reserve chute. I was glad that he knew automatically what to do, rather than having to create a solution on the fly, pun intended. After we finally got the secondary chute opened, we had had a freefall of over 10,000 feet – which was great value for the money. Upon landing, he jokingly told me that he would have to charge me for two chutes! (cont'd)

Training needs to be managed well so that you don't create additional risks. In New Zealand a number of years back, a tragic accident very nearly took place when some hunters stumbled into an Army unit's practice ambush drill. The Army was expecting an enemy disguised as local insurgents, so they opened fire on the unsuspecting hunters with blanks. The hunters, thinking they were under live fire and fearing for their lives, opened up with real bullets.

You will probably never face the extremes of combat, but there may be lessons you can learn for handling infrequent but high-consequence situations. You may not be able to anticipate or train for the specifics of every situation. There are, however, ways to build capabilities in individuals, teams, and organizations to react under the fire of public or regulatory attention.

How might competitors ambush your company? How can you prepare in advance?

When I trained the Australian Army counter-ambush drill was to run into the direction of the attack, as a team, with maximum firepower.

Do you know that your people will stand up in a firefight and head in the right direction? Have you trained people in the actions they need to take?

Experience also affects our response capabilities, partly by creating mental models that can guide future actions, either for good or harm. Laurence Gonzales said: "The word 'experienced' often refers to someone who's gotten away with doing the wrong thing more frequently than you have."

Establish systems, for example, a "Golden Goose" award, to reduce fear and promote sharing of lessons learned.

Our ability to estimate risks accurately depends partly on perception. For example, our brains are wired to respond more strongly to exceptional, fast events, such as a plane crash, rather than the far more prevalent risks of smoking, poor diet, and lack of exercise.

Risk is relative but also perceived. Some of the fear related to change and crises is that you do not always know where the bottom is. Investor behavior during the financial crisis of 2008 illustrates this.

In New Zealand, I once thought I was going to be swept out to sea and drowned. I had swum across a glacier-fed river in the morning to go on a hike near the Hollyford River. Late in the afternoon, when I was already tired from hiking, I went to swim back. By then, the river was much higher, which is a common pattern in the mountains there. I am a decent swimmer, but I was swept downstream faster than I expected. The problem was that I was close to where the river emptied into the ocean, and the river broadened the further I was swept down.

The cold started to get into my muscles, and my legs started cramping. I kicked harder to stay warm, but I just kept getting swept further downstream. My legs started to feel like lead and began dropping below the surface – a bad sign. Turning back was not an option. I got quite worried as my legs lost more and more of their power, and I started sinking. As I did, I touched the bottom. I was standing on a sandbank.

Although it was about 50 yards to the other side, I found that the sandbank extended all the way, so I was able to wade across. I still had an eight-mile hike back to camp, but I was able to warm up by jogging until I found a farmer's cabin with the light on. While I was drinking some tea, the farmer told me he was a local search and rescue member and recounted that two other people had drowned recently while trying to get across on horses. Appropriately, he tore strips off me.

Be honest with people about the risks when change is in the air. Don't try to protect them by sugarcoating or being overly optimistic.

Knowing where the bottom is can help people create a stop-loss on worry and decide whether they want to venture into the stream or play it safe and stay on shore.

Crisis Analysis

Crises can happen quickly in business, but they can happen even more quickly in outdoor contexts. If you catch an edge in an eddy, your kayak can be flipped in seconds, leaving you out of air, upside down, and heading downstream for the next rapid. If you hit an ice patch when you are driving, your car can suddenly be sliding sideways into oncoming traffic. At such times, there is a tremendous tendency to overreact or act immediately. But in almost every situation, it is better to take a few seconds or even fractions of a second to put on your PFD©.

A PFD©, a personal flotation device, is used while sailing, kayaking, or rafting to keep you buoyant if you are suddenly dumped into the water. It buys you time to assess your situation and determine your next steps. I use the acronym to remind me to *pause, focus,* and *decide.* Pause, even for a microsecond, to gain situational awareness. Focus to decide which situational factors to prioritize. Then decide on the best course of action. When your car slides on ice, for example, it's helpful to avoid the tendency to react immediately by slamming on the brakes, which only exacerbates the situation.

Use the PFD approach when you are suddenly hit with bad news.

Part of the crisis-analysis phase should include examining whether a situation is a threat or an opportunity. The Chinese symbol for crisis and opportunity is the same. Lifeguards frequently warn people to stay away from rips and even put up flags to indicate their locations. Boardriders, on the other hand, view the rips as elevators to get them beyond the shore break and into the takeoff zone.

If you can adapt and take advantage of a situation, you may have a temporary competitive advantage while others have to shut down their operations. If you have cash flow reserves, you can pick up assets cheaply when the economy overall is tanking.

Useful tools for crisis management. Some useful tools for crisis management in both the outdoors and business include:

Triage. Triage is a process of prioritizing resources to accident victims who can be saved or are the most essential to the organization's survival. It's a common strategy when downsizing an organization.

Chain of events analysis. What are the number and type of linked events that could escalate risks? For example, if you lose a key account, what will the likely impact be on other accounts?

Margins assessment. How much variation in environmental conditions would it take to turn the situation ugly? For example, if you are a high-cost oil shale producer, how long can you hold out while OPEC keeps their prices low?

Risk/reward ratio. What are you risking for a potential gain, for example, in a particular financial investment?

Resources inventory. What is in your backpack? What is your cash flow situation? What competencies and physical resources does your organization have available to help weather, for example, a competitor's campaign to slash prices?

Another framework for helping people deal with change, which I have labeled SCC/VVR© (speed, complexity, control/vision, values, relationships), came from an unlikely direction. I was interviewing people examining spiritual disciplines and tools for handling change when I found some patterns that seem to cut across all religious and non-religious disciplines. Three main factors seem to influence the amount of felt change that people experience:

1. The *speed* at which the change is occurring

2. The *complexity* of the changes (number and degree of interconnectedness)

3. The amount of *control* people feel they have over the changes (for example, whether they are initiating the change or the change is imposed on them)

Help employees during times of change by managing the pace of change and testing that people are not becoming saturated with change. Where possible, give people some choice in the timing and sequence of changes. Help people find as much stability as possible.

In my research, three main factors emerged that promote a sense of stability for people faced with significant change: consistent vision, values, and relationships. Explore how the change can support your personal or organizational vision. Just because the way you do things changes (for example, with the introduction of new software), it doesn't mean that the values are shifting. It may simply mean an increased focus on excellence.

Change can damage relationships. Take time to nurture your relationships both at and outside work.

Response

Individuals, teams, and organizations have a range of conscious and unconscious responses or choices to the crises they encounter. In both corporate and outdoors settings, the choices survivors make are affected by a wide range of physical, emotional, social, and psychological factors.

When Laurence Gonzales wrote *Deep Survival*, he examined, in a range of riveting survival stories, who lives, who dies, and why.[49] These were some of the factors and skills he identified:

- A reason, or people, to live for
- Self-control
- Adaptability
- The skill of environmental scanning
- Avoiding impulsive behavior
- Humility
- Rapid learning

---

[49]   Gonzales, L. (2003). *Deep Survival: Who Lives, Who Dies and Why.* New York, NY: W.W. Norton & Company.

- Ability to take counterintuitive action
- Accurate mental models
- Appropriate use of emotions
- Transferable experience
- Turning fear into focus[50]

Freeze, fight, or flight. A common way to categorize responses is by freeze, fight, or flight. Freeze is a response used by some animals to take advantage of natural camouflage. True freezing with a cognitive or a physical lockup has less application for managing an outdoors or organizational crisis, since it leaves the victim subject to external forces.

Flight is appropriate in some circumstances, for example, in exiting a partnership with a supplier who poses a legal or ethical liability, or exiting a market because of emerging competition or changing demographics.

On Mount Dixon in New Zealand, my climbing partner and I belayed up steep slopes in the morning because the ice was hard. When we descended in the afternoon, we took off the ropes and moved as quickly as we could because the snow was softening rapidly, which increased the risk of avalanche. If an avalanche had broken beneath us, we would have had to go into fight mode very quickly, "log rolling" to the side if possible.

A variation of the freeze response is the withdrawal response. I once worked in a program for youth at risk on an island off the shores of New Zealand for 31 days. A fishing boat was to bring the facilitators and the court-referred youth to the island. On our way, we encountered a significant storm with waves much higher than radio masts coming at us from every direction. We could not turn around because we risked being swamped. But the captain did drop the speed significantly when we rolled dramatically over to one side with just inches of freeboard remaining. It was a dangerous situation. Later, we learned that a sailboat went down in the same area with loss of life. (cont'd)

---

[50]   Ibid.

I chose to ride out the storm at the stern in spite of the weather. At one point, a kayak we had lashed to the roof broke free, and I grabbed it just before it went overboard. Another time, a particularly big wave broke over the bow and swept two program participants along the gunnels towards the stern where I was able to grab them. They retreated downstairs.

Perhaps the outside was not the safest place for me to be, but the area below the decks where most people had withdrawn was a nightmare. Every one of the 36 people on the boat that day, except for the captain and I, was seasick. When I was on deck, I at least felt like I was actively fighting the storm, even if I was only fighting for my balance. Down below, everyone had withdrawn into victim mode.

Similar patterns occur during organizational change. Employees may withdraw, hunker down, and wait for the axe to fall.

Don't let your employees fall into victim mode. Help them find even small ways in which they can influence or control the events around them.

Managers, knowing they will have to deliver bad news, may become reclusive, emotionless automatons. At such times, leaders need to step out of themselves and provide more communication, more authenticity, and more candor than ever.

A fight response can involve either cognitive or physical capacities. Business examples of different fight responses would include reviewing strategies to adapt to market changes and improving work flow processes (cognitive) and ramping up oil production to retain market share (physical).

"Cowboy up" is a bull-riding term that speaks to courage, character, and taking responsibility. Cowboy up is the moment you sit on the bull's back and prepare for whatever comes. Learning to ride bulls, one of the things I remember most clearly, was the emphasis the cowboys placed on personal accountability and never giving up. Even if the bull gores you, you run, walk, or crawl to get out of the way rather than just lying there waiting for the rodeo clowns to rescue you. Each time the clowns have to step in, they place their lives at risk; they are the unsung heroes in rodeo. One cowboy proudly told the story of a rider who had been gored but managed to drag himself out of the arena, just past the chutes, before he died of internal injuries.

Control or adapt? Life is not fair. Things you can't predict or control will happen. Sometimes it makes sense to try to control a situation. Other times it makes sense to adapt to it.

> Learning to ride bulls was a humbling experience. I was naively self-confident, and since I was in pretty good shape, I did not think it would be very difficult to stay on a bull for eight seconds.
>
> After the training phase, I had the opportunity to ride eight bulls over two days. I came to the arena with a take-charge attitude, which was patently absurd given the 800 to 1,000 pounds of muscled animals I was attempting to control. My inability to control the animals should have become apparent as soon as I entered the chute and adrenaline started flooding into my system. But it lasted a few more seconds as I got dumped unceremoniously on my butt eight times in a row. The bulls slashed at me in the chutes, stomped on me when I hit the ground, and rolled me in the mud with their horns for good measure. It should have been enough to make me rethink my approach. Stubbornness has its place, but it can also get in the way of learning.

Where are you trying to achieve results through stubbornness rather than through learning?

> Cowboys often see bull riding as character development. Not that I was really a bull rider; for the bulls I was just a scratching post and something they could use to wipe the mud off their hooves.
>
> (cont'd)

I received some strong guidance from a grizzled old cowboy on Day 3. He said to me: "Son, you're pretty cocky. You think you can control those bulls, eh?" At the end of the long weekend, we had the opportunity to review a videotape of our rides. That was when his advice finally started to sink in. On each ride, it was clear that I had attempted to control the animal rather than staying in balance, focusing on my seat, and going with the flow. My arrogant attempts at control had simply made it easier for the bull to throw me off.

Mental toughness is an asset, but that doesn't mean being inflexible. In some types of crises, it makes more sense to adapt than try to control the situation. Attempting to over-control things as a leader often leads to people kicking back.

How are you impacting people when you take the reins and refuse to let anyone else have control?

Stubbornness and lack of flexibility are common results of early success. Marshal Goldsmith, the top-ranked executive coach, titled one of his books *What Got You Here Won't Get You There*. In the mountains, the route that got you to the top one year may be blocked the next.

Overconfidence. Executives who reach the top often have a very strong belief in their capabilities, which is probably necessary. Overconfidence, though, in one's power, whether physical or mental, can translate into intellectual arrogance, lack of flexibility, and inappropriate risk-taking. Highly competitive leaders can create additional risks and exposure for their companies when they invest their egos too far and refuse to back down from what should be purely a business decision.

Where might you have become too confident, rigid, or intellectually arrogant?

Overconfidence nearly got my climbing partners and me into big trouble on Mount Sealy, my second climb. Glissading (skiing downhill on your boots) is a fun activity but potentially very dangerous if not done in control. Descending from the summit of Mount Sealy, there is a snow gully that provides a fast descent route. Trevor went first. James and I followed later, choosing to drink some water and gobble down a snack before heading down.

Forgetting all advice to glissade under control, James and I got into a competition on the way down trying to see who could go fastest. We hit a patch of ice and suddenly took off, losing our ability to slow down in spite of our attempts to self-arrest by digging in our axes. Thesno w slope ran out ending in gravel and rock. Trevor was in complete control and just yards away from stopping when I slammed into him and dragged him along the gravel for 25 feet before we came to a halt, fortunately, unharmed. Not my proudest moment.

James hit the gravel a few yards to our right and went airborne for about 20 feet, tumbling in the air. He slammed into the rocks, and I was sure there would be a major accident. But we were extremely fortunate, and all we had to deal with was a large can of baked beans that had exploded inside James' pack. Lesson learned.

Make sure you are competing in appropriate places.

Recovery

Be prepared for survivor guilt after a crisis such as a downsizing.

It can sap the productivity out of people just when you need it the most.

Start the recovery process early by encouraging people to take ownership in rebuilding after the crisis. Let people mourn and remind them why you chose them as survivors. You may be busy with business issues, but continue to check in with people to assess their progress towards recovery.

People are your source of productivity.

Don't be a victim. Use the lulls between storms to train and prepare for harsher weather.

When a storm hits, protect yourself and others by ensuring that you are scanning the environment for potential changes. Are those changes going to be an opportunity or threat?

Help people through the recovery, not just the immediate crisis.

Small Steps

1. *Help your organization become good at predicting storms.*

2. *Create contingency plans ahead of time for addressing crises.*

3. *Build capacity for adapting to unforeseen circumstances through first-principles thinking (Elon Musk), general crisis management training, and identifying transferable competencies.*

4. *Know what resources are available in your team and externally, and know how to access them.*

5. *Tap into historical knowledge to identify potential solutions for crises that have precedents.*

CHAPTER 11

Your Next Adventure

Expeditions can be challenging, but leaving home can also be very hard. It is tough to leave your comfortable space and the friends you love for unknown places, rough living conditions, and uncertain outcomes. Commercial adventures can be expensive, and all adventures at minimum take time away from other responsibilities.

For others, returning may be the hardest part of a journey. The view from the summit can be exhilarating; a week spent paddling a wilderness river washes away the concerns of daily life. Returning home can seem mundane.

So why set out for potential hardships in the first place? Why not watch it all on the Red Bull or National Geographic Channels from the comfort of a recliner, beer in hand, in a temperature-controlled room? Very few of us are professional adventurers. For most of us, adventure is training for real life. The biggest value in heading out may be in the lessons we learn and share with others about leading our friends, our peers, our teams, or ourselves.

My life lessons have often had parallels in my adventures. The only marathon I have run, for example, I completed in 2 hours and 58 minutes, which is a pretty decent time. However, I could have finished even more quickly if I had paced myself correctly. I took off quickly, lost some momentum in the middle of the race, and sprinted at 80% of my maximum at the finish. Since I had not done any training runs longer than 55 minutes, I did not realize I still had gas in the tank. I notice the same pattern with projects – I start fast, lose some momentum in the middle, and finish very strongly.

What are you learning from life's adventures? Here are some tips to leverage your experiences.

Know What Drives You

Knowing what drives your sense of adventure, regardless of what form it takes, can help you learn more from the experience and share the lessons more effectively with others.

My first survival expedition occurred when I left home at age six. Looking back, I suspect my parents were not that surprised. A few weeks prior, I had undertaken a training expedition. On my first day of school, at lunchtime, I had walked three miles home, unaccompanied, to play with the kids next door. The search and rescue mission was called off when Mum spotted me 18 feet up in one of the neighbor's trees.

This time, I was headed walkabout for real. I had fought with Mum during a day off from school and decided that living off the land would be preferable to living in misery at home. (The world can seem incredibly unfair to a six-year-old). We lived only a few miles from Sydney's Royal National Park, so I packed a little red wagon with supplies, swung a tiny backpack over my shoulders, and headed off. In my wagon, I had vegemite and carrot sandwiches, some tiny packs of sultanas, some matches, and an Aboriginal fishing spear I had made that morning from an old broom handle. The rocks along the national park waterfront would provide oysters. I already knew how to catch small lizards, so I planned to impale some of them on sharpened sticks and roast them over a fire. I had seen small creeks running into the bay while on a family fishing trip, so I knew I could get fresh water.

For some reason, Dad came home early that day (I still wonder if Mum gave him a call). I was only about 100 yards from home when he pulled up beside me in his car. He sat down at the side of the road and listened to my plans. He marveled at my fishing spear, which would undoubtedly help me land some "big ones," and he commiserated that, yes, life could certainly be unfair. He did wonder, though, whether having some money might help me be able to travel further afield if I should want to. Would it make sense to earn a little money at home first? So my sense of injustice and hurt faded. I learned you could make money from traveling, and my parents got their son back for another 12 years until I joined the Army. Given the grief I have often put them through, I wonder who got the best deal.

Hopefully, we seek adventure for more positive reasons.

My 550-mile winter mountain-biking trip down the Yukon River was born from one key desire. At the time, I was working professionally as an Outward Bound instructor and wanted to remind myself what it was like for program participants to step out of their comfort zone, as we frequently encouraged them to do. It was a personal opportunity to practice leading by example. Since I was biking solo, I would only be leading myself, but I think that is the best place to start a leadership journey anyway. We lead from the inside out.

Whether it is a new leadership role or an adventure in the outdoors, know why you are setting out. It will help you stay motivated when things get tough, and it will also maximize your learning.

I have always been very forward-looking. However, as I get older, the element of uncertainty in adventure and life encourages me more and more to enjoy the journey, not just the summit. We are not promised tomorrow, only this moment. Mountaintop memories, while holding meaning for years, are brief and fleeting. After having invested tens of thousands of dollars and climbed hundreds of thousands of feet training for Mount Everest, I only spent 20 minutes on the summit. As Robert Pirsig said: "To live only for some future goal is shallow. It's the sides of the mountain that sustain life, not the top."

Take time to recover, rest, and learn before you set out on your next adventure.

In most of the companies I have worked with, projects follow each other like a series of breaking waves. Surfers know it is tiring to keep paddling out when the waves keep breaking over their heads. Build time into workflows to learn and recover before paddling out for the next wave. Take time to celebrate the last great ride. Learn from the last wave of projects, and share that learning.

Thank your sponsors.

Brand ambassadors and professional adventurers know the importance of thanking sponsors and supporters when they return. The glory may go to the project leader, guides, and the front-line troops, but it is the Sherpas and the rear-echelon support staff that enable big projects to move forward. If you want them to be there for you next time, make sure they feel recognized and appreciated this time.

Promote Discovery

My most enjoyable adventures have had an element of exploration and discovery, whether it was a discovery about myself, or a sense of an actual physical discovery. Here are a few examples: a cave chamber in Tasmania that no one else had been able to squeeze into before, a canyon that probably less that 50 people had descended at the time, and an 80-foot long waterfall in Borneo that has only been seen by the local Penan people and a handful of Westerners.

Most of the world is mapped now, but the human experience still has large blank spots to be explored. Even in organizations where the emphasis is on efficiency, repeatability, and stability, there are still things to discover about how we work and interact with others.

What is the discovery edge for you or your organization?

Bring the adventure back. As one HR manager put it: "today employees don't want a career, they want an experience."[51]

For many, adventures are peak experiences. Hopefully, one of the things you take away from your adventures is an increased desire to shape a workplace into a meaningful life experience for your employees. I hope this book has offered some small steps you can take to achieve that. Great journeys at work can be designed and executed in the same way as expeditions.

---

[51] Bersin, J. (2014, March 15). *Why Companies Fail To Engage Today's Workforce*: The Overwhelmed Employee. Retrieved May 14, 2015, from http://www.forbes.com/sites/joshbersin/2014/03/15/why-companies-fail-to-engage-todays-workforce-the-overwhelmed-employee/

Whether it's a story or a multi-media presentation, *find a way to pass on the value of adventure to others.*

An Australian aboriginal proverb says: "We are all visitors to this time, this place. We are just passing through. Our purpose here is to observe, to learn, to grow, to love... and then we return home." "Adventure is only a state of mind" (Alastair Humphreys), so how can we encourage a spirit of adventure and exploration in our workplaces, communities, and organizations?

- *Ask employees what brings adventure or excitement to their work.*
- *Say yes more often.*
- *Volunteer in a field that is new to you.*
- *Set a goal of doing something different once a year.*
- *Travel in a way that forces you to learn from other cultures.*
- *Set out on a local expedition. Search out people who are successful in their fields and interview them. What can you transfer to your workplace?*
- *Set up an exploration fund at work just for developing new ideas. Recipients may travel to other countries, companies, or industries to explore what they are doing. The person traveling must provide a slideshow upon return.*
- *Set up an "Adventurer of the Year" award.*

What is the scale of your next adventure?

Shelli Johnson runs a company called Your Epic Life. It weaves transformational coaching into soul-searching wilderness journeys. On the other end of the spectrum, Alastair Humphreys promotes the idea of "microadventures": "Simple expeditions and challenges which are close to home, affordable and easy to organize [,] [...] short, and yet very effective [...] [with] the spirit [...] of a big adventure. [...] A microadventure can be anything that feels fresh, new and challenging for you."[52]

---

[52]   Humphreys, A. (n.d.). Microadventures. Retrieved January 27, 2016, from http://www.alastairhumphreys.com/books/microadventures/

An aboriginal proverb says, "Those who lose dreaming are lost." So what is your dream? What is calling you now? Where is the next adventure for you? Is it stepping out with that creative idea you have been nurturing and protecting for too long? Is it pushing your boat out into the stream and taking on the turbulence of starting a business of your own? Is it trying a new way of relating with your partner or an important colleague? "The journey of a thousand miles begins with a single step," (Lao Tzu) and "Today is your day! Your mountain is waiting. So... get on your way" (Dr. Seuss).

About the Author

Having grown up in Australia and New Zealand, Steve Camkin now makes his home in Boise, Idaho, where he can be found skiing, mountain biking, kayaking, or volunteering in Idaho's Mountain Search and Rescue Team. Steve is the founder of Three Peaks Consulting LLC, an alliance of global leadership and organizational development professionals who strive together to "Make some money, have some fun, and do some good."

In *High Altitude Leadership: Small Steps to Get You to the Top of Big Mountains*, Steve shares hard-earned lessons learned and practical tips from leadership roles in the corporate jungle and wilderness expeditions over 35 years on seven continents.

Steve's broad life experiences bridge the worlds of corporations, nonprofits, the military, and adventure. He has held leadership positions in multinational corporations, has a Ph.D. in Human and Organizational Systems, was an Outward Bound instructor for seven years leading teams on expeditions up to 42 days in length, and has completed numerous international expeditions in jungles, on the ocean, on whitewater, and in deserts. In 2015, he completed The Seven Summits – the highest peaks on each continent.

Contact Information:
Email: threepeaksconsultingllc@gmail.com
Website: three-peaks-consulting.com